BAPTISTWAYPRESS®

Adult Bible Study Guide

The Gospel of Mark

*Jesus' Works
and Words*

Ellis Orozco
Mark Denison
Phil Lineberger

BAPTISTWAYPRESS®

Dallas, Texas

The Gospel of Mark: Jesus' Works and Words—Adult Bible Study Guide—Large Print

Copyright © 2007 by BAPTISTWAY PRESS®.
All rights reserved.
Printed in the United States of America.

BAPTISTWAY PRESS® Management Team
Executive Director, Baptist General Convention of Texas: Charles Wade
Director, Missions, Evangelism, and Ministry Team: Wayne Shuffield
Ministry Team Leader: Phil Miller
Publisher, BAPTISTWAY PRESS®: Ross West

Cover and Interior Design and Production: Desktop Miracles, Inc.
Printing: Data Reproductions Corporation
Cover Photo: The Sea of Galilee, istockphoto.com

First edition: December 2007
ISBN:1–931060–97–5

How to Make the Best Use of This Issue

Whether you're the teacher or a student—
1. Start early in the week before your class meets.
2. Overview the study. Review the table of contents and read the study introduction. Try to see how each lesson relates to the overall study.
3. Use your Bible to read and consider prayerfully the Scripture passages for the lesson. (You'll see that each writer has chosen a favorite translation for the lessons in this issue. You're free to use the Bible translation you prefer and compare it with the translation chosen for that unit, of course.)
4. After reading all the Scripture passages in your Bible, then read the writer's comments. The comments are intended to be an aid to your study of the Bible.
5. Read the small articles—"sidebars"—in each lesson. They are intended to provide additional, enrichment information and inspiration and to encourage thought and application.
6. Try to answer for yourself the questions included in each lesson. They're intended to encourage further thought and application, and they can also be used in the class session itself.

If you're the teacher—
A. Do all of the things just mentioned, of course.
As you begin the study with your class, be sure
to find a way to help your class know the date on
which each lesson will be studied. You might do
this in one or more of the following ways:

- In the first session of the study, briefly
overview the study by identifying with your
class the date on which each lesson will be
studied. Lead your class to write the date in
the table of contents on page 9 and on the
first page of each lesson. *Note*: A Christmas
lesson is included. If your class uses the
Christmas lesson, you may need to decide
how to study the other lessons, such as by
combining two lessons or studying the missed
lesson at a special class meeting.
- Make and post a chart that indicates the date
on which each lesson will be studied.
- If all of your class has e-mail, send them
an e-mail with the dates the lessons will be
studied.
- Provide a bookmark with the lesson dates.
You may want to include information about
your church and then use the bookmark as a
visitation tool, too.
- Develop a sticker with the lesson dates, and
place it on the table of contents or on the back
cover.

How to Make the Best Use of This Issue

B. Get a copy of the *Teaching Guide*, a companion piece to this *Study Guide*. The *Teaching Guide* contains additional Bible comments plus two teaching plans. The teaching plans in the *Teaching Guide* are intended to provide practical, easy-to-use teaching suggestions that will work in your class.

C. After you've studied the Bible passage, the lesson comments, and other material, use the teaching suggestions in the *Teaching Guide* to help you develop your plan for leading your class in studying each lesson.

D. You may want to get the additional adult Bible study comments—*Adult Online Bible Commentary*—by Dr. Jim Denison, pastor of Park Cities Baptist Church, Dallas, Texas, that are available at www.baptistwaypress.org and can be downloaded free. An additional teaching plan plus teaching resource items are also available at www.baptistwaypress.org.

E. You also may want to get the enrichment teaching help that is provided on the internet by the *Baptist Standard* at www.baptiststandard.com. (Other class participants may find this information helpful, too.) Call 214–630–4571 to begin your subscription to the printed edition of the *Baptist Standard*.

F. Enjoy leading your class in discovering the meaning of the Scripture passages and in applying these passages to their lives.

Writers of This Study Guide

Ellis Orozco, the writer of unit 1, lessons 1–3, is pastor of Calvary Baptist Church, McAllen, Texas. He is a graduate of Texas A & M in mechanical engineering and of Southwestern Baptist Theological Seminary.

Mark Denison wrote unit 2, lessons 4–7, and the Christmas lesson. Dr. Denison is pastor of First Baptist Church, Gainesville, Texas. He is a graduate of Houston Baptist University and Southwestern Baptist Theological Seminary (M.Div., D.Min.).

Phil Lineberger, the writer of unit 3, lessons 8–13, is pastor of Williams Trace Baptist Church, Sugar Land, Texas. Dr. Lineberger has served as president of the Baptist General Convention of Texas. He is a graduate of The University of Arkansas and of Southwestern Baptist Theological Seminary (M. Div., D.Min.).

The Gospel of Mark: Jesus' Works and Words

U N I T   T H R E E

With Jesus on the Way to the Cross

Introducing

THE GOSPEL OF MARK: Jesus' Works and Words

No matter how good our motivation is, we likely do not approach the Gospel of Mark with the same level of interest, and certainly not the same sense of urgency, that those who first read it did. For one thing, we likely think we already know much of the story of Jesus. So now we're just going over it one more time. It will be good to do that, we're sure, but we're really pretty familiar with it, we think.

And, do we have a sense of urgency about our Christian faith? Probably not. Mark's first readers, though, lived in threatening and difficult days. They may have been facing persecution in Rome during the middle and latter part of the decade of the 60s. In such a situation, they needed to know what kind of person and message could demand their devotion even to the point of giving their lives. We—particularly North American Christians—though, tend to live more or less comfortable lives. Many seem to think they should get some sort of prize for discipleship just because they attend church fairly regularly.

If these are our thoughts, we're mistaken. We've likely not absorbed fully the challenging nature of who Jesus is. Likely, too, we've not caught up to Jesus' demands of those who would be his disciples, and we've ignored Jesus' call to us to participate in his mission in our world.

The Gospel of Mark presents Jesus as being radically different from what people of his day expected. Once we get to know Jesus as the Gospel of Mark presents him, we may well think that that's still the case.

The first verse of Mark describes Jesus as "Christ, the Son of God" (Mark 1:1). The rest of the Gospel of Mark verifies and clarifies in many ways what that means—not just theologically but personally. Be prepared to affirm or re-affirm what that means for you as you study these lessons.

Studying the Gospel of Mark

Unit one, "Good News Today," is a three-lesson study of Mark 1:1—3:6. The first lesson focuses on Mark 1:1–20, "Let Me Introduce Jesus." Included are passages on John the Baptist's preparations for Jesus' coming; Jesus' baptism; Jesus' experience of temptation in the wilderness; the beginning of Jesus' proclamation of the good news; and the call of the first four disciples and their response. Lesson two provides a study of Mark 2:1–11, "A Faith Worth Acting On." It emphasizes the kind of faith Jesus' authority calls forth—a faith that acts. Lesson three, on Mark 2:13–17, 23—3:6, is titled, "Live the Unbound Life." It focuses on how Jesus supersedes all religious and cultural rules and traditions.

Unit two, "Showing Who Jesus Is," begins with Jesus departing "with his disciples to the sea" (Mark 3:7) after his initial ministry. The section extends to the midpoint of Mark's Gospel near the end of chapter 8. In this section, Jesus further established his identity as "Christ the Son of God" (1:1) by demonstrating his authority in numerous ways.

Unit three, "With Jesus on the Way to the Cross," follows Jesus and his disciples from Jesus' challenging question, "But who do you say that I am?" (8:29), to the cross and the resurrection. The emphasis of the passages selected for study is on the kind of discipleship to which Jesus calls his followers. These lessons aim at helping us to consider more specifically—for us—what Jesus meant when he said, "If any want to become my followers, let them deny themselves and take up their cross and follow me" (8:34).

Note: The time of the first release of these materials includes the Christmas holiday. To meet the needs of churches who wish to have an emphasis on Christmas at this time, a Christmas lesson is included.

UNIT ONE. GOOD NEWS TODAY

THE GOSPEL OF MARK: *Jesus' Works and Words*

UNIT TWO. SHOWING WHO JESUS IS

Lesson 4	More Than Meets the Eye	Mark 4:21–34
Lesson 5	Jesus and Hopeless Situations	Mark 4:35—5:43
Lesson 6	When Cleanliness Is Not Next to Godliness	Mark 7:1–23
Lesson 7	There Are None So Blind	Mark 8:11–26

UNIT THREE. WITH JESUS ON THE WAY TO THE CROSS

Lesson 8	Not an Easy Way	Mark 8:27–38
Lesson 9	Me First	Mark 9:30–37
Lesson 10	Disciple = Servant	Mark 10:32–45
Lesson 11	Discipleship in Dangerous Times	Mark 13:1–13, 32–37
Lesson 12	Not Me	Mark 14:10–31
Lesson 13	The Worst and Best of Times	Mark 14:61b–64; 15:9–24, 37–41; 16:1–8
Christmas Lesson	Glory to God!	Luke 2:1–20

Additional Resources for Studying the Gospel of Mark:[1]

William Barclay. *The Gospel of Mark*. Revised edition. Philadelphia: The Westminster Press, 1975.

James A. Brooks. *Mark*. The New American Commentary. Volume 23. Nashville, Tennessee: Broadman Press, 1991.

Sharyn Dowd. *Reading Mark: A Literary and Theological Commentary on the Second Gospel*. Reading the New Testament Series. Macon, Georgia: Smyth and Helwys Publishing, 2000.

David E. Garland. *Mark*. The NIV Application Commentary. Grand Rapids, Michigan: Zondervan Publishing House, 1996.

Craig S. Keener. *IVP Bible Background Commentary: New Testament*. Downers Grove, Illinois: InterVarsity Press, 1993.

William L. Lane. *The Gospel According to Mark*. The New International Commentary on the New Testament. Grand Rapids, Michigan: William B. Eerdmans Publishing Company, 1974.

Lloyd J. Ogilvie. *Life Without Limits*: Waco, Texas: Word Books, Publisher, 1975.

Pheme Perkins. "Mark." *The New Interpreter's Bible*, Volume VIII. Nashville, Tennessee: Abingdon Press, 1995.

A. T. Robertson. *Word Pictures in the New Testament*. Volume I. Nashville, Tennessee: Broadman Press, 1930.

NOTES

1. Listing a book does not imply full agreement by the writers or BAPTISTWAY with all of its comments.

Good News Today

Unit one, "Good News Today," is a three-lesson study of Mark 1:1—3:6. The first lesson focuses on Mark 1:1–20, "Let Me Introduce Jesus." Included are passages on John the Baptist's preparations for Jesus' coming; Jesus' baptism; Jesus' experience of temptation in the wilderness; the beginning of Jesus' proclamation of the good news; and the call of the first four disciples and their response.

Lesson two provides a study of Mark 2:1–11, "A Faith Worth Acting On." It emphasizes the kind of faith Jesus' authority calls forth—a faith that acts.

Lesson three, on Mark 2:13–17, 23—3:6, is titled, "Live the Unbound Life." It focuses on how Jesus supersedes all religious and cultural rules and traditions.[1]

17

THE GOSPEL OF MARK: *Jesus' Works and Words*

These lessons and these Scripture passages will call us to remember and live our lives on the basis of a truth even religious people often seem to forget. The gospel is *good news* in a world—even the religious world—that seems full of bad news.

UNIT ONE. GOOD NEWS TODAY

Lesson 1	Let Me Introduce Jesus	Mark 1:1–20
Lesson 2	A Faith Worth Acting On	Mark 2:1–12
Lesson 3	Live the Unbound Life	Mark 2:13–17, 23—3:6

NOTES

1. Unless otherwise indicated, all Scripture quotations are from the New International Version.

Main Idea

Jesus, whose identity as Christ and Son of God was verified in many ways, came proclaiming God's good news and calling people to follow him.

Question to Explore

If we knew nothing about Jesus before reading this passage, what would it tell us about him?

Let Me Introduce Jesus

Study Aim

To state what this passage tells us about Jesus and the response it calls us to make

Study and Action Emphases

- Affirm the Bible as our authoritative guide for life and ministry
- Share the gospel with all people
- Develop a growing, vibrant faith

Quick Read

Mark introduces Jesus and verifies his identity from multiple sources. It then establishes Jesus' purpose on earth and shows the authority with which Jesus came.

Have you ever been to a movie and within ten minutes discovered that you wasted your money? You kept watching just in case something started happening in the movie. After twenty minutes with no action, you were ready to bolt for the door. In fact, if your seat had not been so comfortable and the popcorn so buttery, you would probably have left the theater and asked for a refund. Why was the movie so boring? The answer is that you watched the screen for twenty minutes and nothing exciting happened.

No one has ever experienced that with the Gospel of Mark. Mark wrote his Gospel like a fast-paced screenplay. The Gospel of Mark hits the ground running from the very beginning. There is more action in the first twenty verses of Mark's Gospel than the first two chapters of most action novels.

In fact, in the first chapter, Mark established Jesus' identity, his purpose on earth, and his authority over humankind. That's not bad for just twenty verses.

Mark 1:1–20

¹The beginning of the gospel about Jesus Christ, the Son of God.
²It is written in Isaiah the prophet:
"I will send my messenger ahead of you,
who will prepare your way"—
³ "a voice of one calling in the desert,

'Prepare the way for the Lord,
  make straight paths for him.'"

4And so John came, baptizing in the desert region and preaching a baptism of repentance for the forgiveness of sins. **5**The whole Judean countryside and all the people of Jerusalem went out to him. Confessing their sins, they were baptized by him in the Jordan River. **6**John wore clothing made of camel's hair, with a leather belt around his waist, and he ate locusts and wild honey. **7**And this was his message: "After me will come one more powerful than I, the thongs of whose sandals I am not worthy to stoop down and untie. **8**I baptize you with water, but he will baptize you with the Holy Spirit."

9At that time Jesus came from Nazareth in Galilee and was baptized by John in the Jordan. **10**As Jesus was coming up out of the water, he saw heaven being torn open and the Spirit descending on him like a dove. **11**And a voice came from heaven: "You are my Son, whom I love; with you I am well pleased."

12At once the Spirit sent him out into the desert, **13**and he was in the desert forty days, being tempted by Satan. He was with the wild animals, and angels attended him.

14After John was put in prison, Jesus went into Galilee, proclaiming the good news of God. **15**"The time has come," he said. "The kingdom of God is near. Repent and believe the good news!"

16As Jesus walked beside the Sea of Galilee, he saw Simon and his brother Andrew casting a net into the lake, for they were fishermen. **17**"Come, follow me,"

Jesus said, "and I will make you fishers of men." [18]At once they left their nets and followed him.

[19]When he had gone a little farther, he saw James son of Zebedee and his brother John in a boat, preparing their nets. [20]Without delay he called them, and they left their father Zebedee in the boat with the hired men and followed him.

Introducing Jesus (1:1–8)

Mark began his Gospel at the beginning of Jesus' ministry. Unlike Matthew and Luke, Mark skipped the birth and childhood of Jesus. He evidently wanted to get right to the action of Jesus' life with his disciples. He used the first twenty verses to introduce the nature of Jesus' ministry and the authority by which Jesus embarked on that ministry.

Mark's opening sentence is most likely the title for the entire work. If Mark were alive today, he would probably not approve of our title for his work— "Mark" or "The Gospel According to Mark." Mark would insist on making the title "The beginning of the gospel about Jesus Christ, the Son of God."

The word "gospel" means *good news*. This word became synonymous with the good news of the salvation that is found in Jesus Christ. In Romans 1:2–4 and 1 Corinthians 15:3–5, Paul indicated that Jesus' death, resurrection, and exaltation comprised the substance of the good news of the early church.

The word "Christ" is the Greek equivalent for the Hebrew word *messiah*, which means *savior*. Mark announced that Jesus was the Messiah for whom the Hebrew people had been waiting.

Mark, in dramatic fashion, used the title "Son of God" as a precursor to the last chapter of his Gospel. There the centurion, standing at the foot of the cross, made the great confession, "Surely this man was the Son of God" (Mark 15:39). These two confessions of Jesus as the Son of God stand as bookends to Mark's Gospel and point to the overarching theme of Mark's work: *Jesus, the Son of God, who has come to save the world.*

After establishing the title for his Gospel account, Mark began the story with a quotation from the Old Testament (1:2–3). He attributed this quotation to the prophet Isaiah, although it is a composite of three Old Testament passages from Exodus, Isaiah, and Malachi (Exodus 23:20; Malachi 3:1; Isaiah 40:3). This composite citation sets the stage for the appearance of John the Baptist and Jesus and appeals to the authority of the prophets for their ministry. The Gospel of Mark seems to be pulling material from the law and the prophets to emphasize the prophetic utterances (in the spirit of Isaiah) that point to the coming Messiah. Perhaps Mark originally quoted the Isaiah passage and later added the other passages from Exodus and Malachi, using only the identifying reference to Isaiah.

> *The Gospel of Mark hits the ground running from the very beginning.*

The Gospel of Mark describes John in a way that tied him to the prophet Elijah. Specific mention of John's clothing woven from camel's hair and his belt made of leather is a direct reference to a similar description of Elijah (Mark 1:6; see 2 Kings 1:8). John the Baptist was the Elijah who was to come preparing the way for the Messiah.

Jesus is the One who comes to take away the sins of the world and provide a permanent solution to sin.

John's message was simple: *Repent, or turn away, from evil* (see Mark 1:4). John's message was one of repentance in order to make the heart ready to receive God. John's call to baptism was not unique in Hebrew history, but John offered the promise of more in the One who was to come.

John promised that One who was greater would come (1:7–8). He was pointing to the Messiah who would baptize with the Holy Spirit. This Messiah who was coming would offer a baptism that was symbolic of a permanent solution to sin.

With his identity, nature, and authority firmly in place, Jesus was ready to embark on his earthly mission.

In the first eight verses, Mark has appealed to the authority of the prophets and the preaching of John the Baptist to introduce Jesus as the Messiah and the Son of God. Jesus is the One who comes to take away the sins of the world and provide a permanent solution to sin.

The Mission (1:9–11)

Jesus came to John the Baptist to be baptized. This event inaugurated Jesus' ministry and mission. It introduced Jesus as a teacher and spiritual leader.

Mark described the baptism in dramatic fashion. "As Jesus was coming up out of the water, he saw heaven being torn open . . ." (1:10). Matthew and Luke described the heavens as being "opened" (Matthew 3:16; Luke 3:21), whereas Mark described the heavens as being "torn open" (a different Greek word). The difference in the Greek words highlights the dramatic tone that Mark created with his Gospel account.

The Spirit settled on Jesus, evidently floating from the heavens the way a dove would fly. Then a voice came from heaven. The voice was that of God the Father, introducing his Son to the world. The voice clearly established Jesus' authority as the Son of God. It was an affirmation of the title of Mark's Gospel (Mark 1:1).

The Father said several important things about his Son. First, the Father identified his relationship with and responsibility for Jesus. He said to Jesus, "You are my Son . . ." (1:11). Jesus' authority and power come from his Father (John 16:23–24). The Father is reflected in his Son (John 14:10). From the beginning God established Jesus as his Son (John 1:1).

The Father also said that he loved Jesus: ". . . whom I love" (Mark 1:11). Jesus is the beloved Son of God. The most amazing aspect to this love is that God's love for Jesus is extended to each of us (John 3:16; 17:23). Every child longs to hear the expression of parental love.

Too, the Father said he was proud of his Son: "with you I am well pleased" (Mark 1:11). The Father loved his Son and was pleased with what Jesus had become. Luke's Gospel reminds us that as a child, Jesus "grew in wisdom and stature, and in favor with God and men" (Luke 2:52). In Mark 1:11 and elsewhere, God the Father placed his stamp of approval on his beloved Son.

Their lives would never be the same, and neither would the world.

The baptism and message from heaven served to initiate Jesus' earthly ministry. Jesus was introduced by the prophets of old, John the Baptist, and even God himself. With his identity, nature, and authority firmly in place, Jesus was ready to embark on his earthly mission. There was only one thing left to do here at the beginning.

The Trial (1:12–13)

Mark, true to form, reported Jesus' wilderness experience in 1:12–13 using only a few words. These words, however, provide a brilliant summary. In two verses, Mark conveyed six key elements that were a part of the temptation experience. They are: (1) the temptation experience happened immediately after the baptism of Jesus; (2) the Holy Spirit led Jesus into the wilderness; (3) Jesus was there for "forty days"; (4) Jesus was "tempted by Satan"; (5) Jesus was exposed to the elements; (6) God's angels took care of Jesus.

Since Matthew, Mark, and Luke recorded the temptation experience, it was obviously a crucial moment in Jesus' life. Jesus had been introduced to the world. It was time for him to be introduced to the enemy. Jesus' authority over the enemy was established in this experience, and God's love and care for him was affirmed.

The Message and the Call (1:14–20)

On returning from the wilderness experience, Jesus immediately began to preach. Mark reported the message that Jesus was preaching. Jesus would instill this message in his disciples.

The message has four parts to it. The first has a strong messianic tone. "The time has come . . ." (Mark 1:15). In the first century, this statement would be perceived as a call to messianic revolution. The Hebrew people had been waiting for another Judas Maccabeus,

Jesus calls all to be his disciples.

a Jewish military leader of the second century B.C., to lead the people away from Roman bondage. Jesus' call to a time that "has come," would be viewed by many as a call to arms. Of course, Jesus had a very different purpose.

Second, Jesus then said, "The kingdom of God is near" (1:15). Again, this was a strong messianic statement. In the mind of the first-century Hebrew, the kingdom of God was the restoration of the throne of David. The kingdom of God was associated with a political revolution. Jesus, however, was speaking in spiritual terms. For Jesus, the kingdom of God was the spiritual rule of God in the life of believers.

Jesus' call is a call to give our lives completely to him, seeking to be like him in every way possible.

Third, Jesus called each person to "repent and believe the good news" (1:15). "Repent" indicates *a willful turning away from sin*. Repentance was the essence of John's message. Jesus, however, added to John's message the important element of *belief* in the good news. *Belief* is the fourth element of the message.

Once Jesus' nature and calling were established, Mark moved to describe the formation of the community who would carry the message.

Andrew had been a disciple of John the Baptist (see John 1:40). John the Baptist told Andrew that Jesus was "the Lamb of God" (John 1:36). Andrew shared the news with Peter, his brother, and they both became Jesus' disciples (John 1:41). Some Bible students propose that the other disciple who was with Andrew in switching his loyalties to Jesus was John, the brother of James (John 1:40). Peter, Andrew, James, and John likely knew each other because they were all fishermen in the Sea of Galilee. The fishing trade in that area was sizable, but it was still a small community by modern standards. Capernaum, for instance, was one of the larger towns along the coast of the Sea of Galilee, and its first-century population is estimated at one thousand at most.

We are to live our lives under the direction and control of the One who came from the Father to save us from our sins.

At the very least, John 1 suggests that before Peter and Andrew heard Jesus say, "Come, follow me" (Mark 1:17), they knew Jesus was a powerful rabbi, associated with John the Baptist, and that John the Baptist had called Jesus "the Lamb of God." This suggestion of prior knowledge of Jesus, however, does not make the call of Jesus in Mark 1:17 any less powerful. Neither does it make the immediate response of Peter and Andrew any less courageous.

Hearing Jesus say, "Come, follow me," was a profound and unforgettable moment in the lives of Peter, Andrew, James, and John. The ramifications of their decision to follow Jesus were just as profound. A student's decision to follow a rabbi meant that the disciple was committing his entire life to that rabbi. Disciples not only wanted to learn from the rabbi, but also they wanted to be just like the rabbi in every way possible.

When Jesus said, "Come, follow me," to Peter, Andrew, James, and John, they immediately recognized this invitation as a privileged call to give their lives completely and irrevocably to Jesus' teachings and way of life. They dropped their nets and followed him. They embarked on a different kind of fishing. Jesus said, "I will make you fishers of men" (Mark 1:17). Their lives would never be the same, and neither would the world.

Implications and Actions

In Mark 1, Mark firmly established Jesus as the Messiah, or Savior, and the Son of God, who came to save us. Mark established this fact through the witness of the Old Testament law and the prophets, the preaching of John the Baptist, the witness of the Heavenly Father, the coming of the Spirit, the leadership of the Spirit, the temptation experience, the preaching of Jesus, and the power of Jesus' call to his disciples.

Jesus calls all to be his disciples. Jesus' call is a call to give our lives completely to him, seeking to be like him in every way possible. This call leads us to drop everything and follow him. We are to live our lives under the direction and control of the One who came from the Father to save us from our sins.

First-Century Hebrew Education

The Hebrew educational system in first-century Palestine included several phases. It began with the home

32

and the synagogue. The culminating phase occurred in the teen years and was reserved for only the most exceptionally gifted students. This study might occur under the leadership of an outstanding rabbi. In this phase the student would study the Old Testament law and its oral interpretation and would learn everything necessary to be a rabbi.

Questions

1. Jesus is the authoritative Son of God. What does that mean for your life? for the lives of your friends?

2. How did the work and preaching of John the Baptist prepare the way for Jesus?

3. What does it mean to *repent?* Have you ever repented of something? How did it feel?

4. Why is it important that the Heavenly Father expressed his love for his Son, Jesus? What does that mean for your life? for the lives of people who are dear to you?

5. Have you accepted Jesus' call on your life? What have been some of the ramifications to that decision?

Focal Text

Mark 2:1–12

Background

Mark 2:1–12

Main Idea

Faith takes action in response to the authority of Jesus.

Question to Explore

Who are you most like in this incident in Jesus' ministry?

LESSON TWO

A Faith Worth Acting On

Study Aim

To decide on at least one way I will act on my faith in Jesus

Study and Action Emphases

- Affirm the Bible as our authoritative guide for life and ministry
- Share the gospel with all people
- Develop a growing, vibrant faith
- Value all people as created in the image of God
- Obey and serve Jesus by meeting physical, spiritual, and emotional needs

Quick Read

Who Jesus is and what Jesus does calls us to exercise our faith by taking bold action to serve Jesus ourselves and bring others to receive the help Jesus provides.

The first chapter of the Gospel of Mark establishes Jesus' authority through the witness of the Old Testament prophets, John the Baptist, and the voice of God. Mark 1 also introduces Jesus' miraculous healing ministry (Mark 1:21–45). Jesus' healing ministry serves as a sign pointing to his authority.

The cumulative effect of all that Mark 1 reports is a portrait of Jesus as one who has unusual authority in his teaching, preaching, and actions. Jesus' fame spread rapidly, and many were coming to him, seeking his help. The incident for study in this lesson is set in this context. This incident shows how at least four people recognized the greatness of Jesus' authority. They placed their faith in what Jesus could do and took action on the basis of that faith to help a friend by bringing him to receive help from Jesus.

Mark 2:1–12

¹A few days later, when Jesus again entered Capernaum, the people heard that he had come home. ²So many gathered that there was no room left, not even outside the door, and he preached the word to them. ³Some men came, bringing to him a paralytic, carried by four of them. ⁴Since they could not get him to Jesus because of the crowd, they made an opening in the roof above Jesus and, after digging through it, lowered the mat the paralyzed man was lying on. ⁵When Jesus saw their faith, he said to the paralytic, "Son, your sins are forgiven."

6Now some teachers of the law were sitting there, thinking to themselves, **7**"Why does this fellow talk like that? He's blaspheming! Who can forgive sins but God alone?"

8Immediately Jesus knew in his spirit that this was what they were thinking in their hearts, and he said to them, "Why are you thinking these things? **9**Which is easier: to say to the paralytic, 'Your sins are forgiven,' or to say, 'Get up, take your mat and walk'? **10**But that you may know that the Son of Man has authority on earth to forgive sins. . . ." He said to the paralytic, **11**"I tell you, get up, take your mat and go home." **12**He got up, took his mat and walked out in full view of them all. This amazed everyone and they praised God, saying, "We have never seen anything like this!"

The Faith of Four Friends

Mark 2:1–12 is the first of five controversies in Mark 2:1—3:6, the other four of which will be studied in the next lesson. These controversies set the stage for Jesus' growing conflict with the Jewish religious establishment. This conflict would lead to the cross.

The opening scene of chapter 2 connects to chapter 1 with the description of the crowd who pressed into the house where Jesus was staying in Capernaum. The house was so full that even the area around the door provided no place even to stand. Jesus was preaching "the word" to them (2:2). "The word" was a synonym for the gospel message that formed the core of Jesus' teaching and preaching.

Some men—at least four—wanted to get into the house to see Jesus. These four were carrying a friend who was paralyzed. When they found it impossible to get into the house because of the crowd, they decided to try the roof. Mediterranean homes were built in such a way as to take advantage of the roof. Many homes had an exterior stairway leading to the roof. The roof was used in the cool of the evening as a place to sit and enjoy the refreshing breeze.

They placed their faith in what Jesus could do and took action on the basis of that faith to help a friend by bringing him to receive help from Jesus.

This setting allowed the four friends to get their friend who was paralyzed to the flat roof of the house in relatively short order. They then began to dig through the thatched roof. The roof probably was made of thatched palm leaves sealed with sun-baked mud. It would not be unreasonably difficult to pull the palm leaves out, digging through the mud that held them in place.

The four men were able to remove enough of the roof so that they could lower their paralyzed friend on his mat through the gaping hole. Jesus saw the four friends lowering the man and commended the friends for their faith (2:5).

The text records no words from the four friends. Jesus saw their action as a wordless request for healing and a practical manifestation of their faith. Jesus affirmed that faith produces an attitude that manifests itself in certain actions. James would later state that faith without action is dead (James 2:17).

A Healing Controversy

Jesus did not immediately heal the paralytic. His first comment on seeing the faith of the four friends was, "Son, your sins are forgiven" (2:5). The "teachers of the law" silently accused Jesus of blasphemy. They rested their accusation on their understanding of the authority of one God. Deuteronomy 6:4 clearly stated the radical monotheistic nature of the Hebrew faith. Here, Jesus was not being accused of claiming to be God but of blaspheming God by claiming to do what only God can do.

> *Jesus affirmed that faith produces an attitude that manifests itself in certain actions.*

Why did Jesus forgive the man's sins before he healed him? There are various opinions as to the answer.

One possibility is that Jesus wanted to deal with the paralytic's spiritual life before he worked on his physical life. This is not to say that the man was paralyzed because of his sins but that his spiritual life was in even more desperate need of healing. Healing the man's limbs would give him a new life on earth. Healing the man's sins would give him new life eternally.

Another explanation is related to the scribes' teaching that this type of physical handicap was a direct result of sin. For example, a man born blind was assumed to have had sinful parents (John 9:1–2). However, here in Mark 2, Jesus forgave the man's sins, and yet the man was still paralyzed. Only later did Jesus heal his physical handicap, thus showing that the two were not connected.

Yet another opinion is that Jesus offered forgiveness of sins to the paralytic because he knew that the scribes would question his authority to do so. He wanted to create a teachable moment for his disciples and the others in the house. He knew that his act would bring the creative tension that would make a lasting impact on everyone in the room. He was right.

Talking about faith can be easy, but actually living out our faith is what is needed.

Jesus understood what was in the hearts of people. He had an ability to discern what people were thinking (Mark 2:8). So Jesus responded to what the scribes were thinking. He took a proactive stance toward those who opposed him. He confronted the questioning hearts, as he often does, with a question of his own. This approach was a common rabbinical method of teaching. He asked his opponents (2:9), "Which is easier?" His question directed the scribes to the question of authority. One who has authority finds it easy to exercise that authority.

42

Jesus then healed the man who was paralyzed (2:10–11). Jesus' action showed in dramatic form the authority he had over the physical world. This action made Jesus' authority clear to all in the room. Those who observed this incident surely were thinking, *If Jesus has the authority to heal a paralytic so easily, perhaps he also has the authority to forgive sins, for such authority can come only from God.* Ultimately, the question that the religious leadership had to answer was: *Is Jesus from God?* This question is the eternal question every person must face and answer.

In Mark 2:10, Jesus offered the reason for the miracle that was to follow. He healed the man who was paralyzed so they might "know that the Son of Man has authority on earth to forgive sins" (2:10). The "teachers of the law" were not questioning the miraculous. Rather they were questioning *Jesus'* authority to perform the miraculous, beginning with his authority to forgive sins.

> *Jesus has everything we need to find restoration in body, mind, and soul.*

Jesus did not expect the scribes to answer his questions, since he immediately turned away from them and toward the man who was paralyzed. Through Jesus' body language, he was saying, *Watch this.*

The room was crowded to capacity with disciples, scribes, and the curious. The four friends were peering down expectantly from the gaping hole in the roof. The paralytic was in the center of the room. Jesus, having asked the piercing question in Mark 2:9, turned his back on his inquisitors. He stretched his hand to the man who was paralyzed and said, "Get up, take your mat and go home." Immediately, the man obeyed, and the crowd gasped in amazement. All of this happened when four friends responded in faith to Jesus' authority.

Implications and Actions

Consider these three principles to be gleaned from this memorable episode in Jesus' Galilean ministry:

(1) The faith of a community has power. Jesus made a point to let the four friends know that it was their faith that brought blessing to their friend. The text does not speak of the level of the faith of the man who was paralyzed. The incident shows us that when our faith is weak, the faith of our friends can help to see us through.

(2) Faith is manifested in action. Neither the four friends nor the man who was paralyzed ever spoke a word to Jesus (or anyone else in the house for that matter). Yet, Jesus saw their actions and called it faith. Talking about faith can be easy, but actually living out our faith is what is needed.

No life issue or crisis is too great for Jesus to handle.

(3) Jesus has authority in both the physical and spiritual realms. He has the authority to forgive

sins. He also has the power to heal the body physically. In short, Jesus has everything we need to find restoration in body, mind, and soul. No life issue or crisis is too great for Jesus to handle.

Through the Roof

Two basic methods existed for constructing flat roofs in first-century Palestine. Many homes used a thatched roof made of palms fastened together and sealed with a mud and straw mixture. The roof of this type of home was not designed to carry much weight.

Some homes had flat roofs composed of large stone tiles that were easy to remove and replace. The tiles were sometimes covered with dirt or sod for insulation purposes. These more affluent homes often had an exterior staircase providing easy access to the roof. Luke's account of the story of the healing of the man who was paralyzed seems to indicate the home had this type of roof (Luke 5:19).

In either case, there was no need to rip up shingles and saw through plywood and beams in order to make a sizable opening in the roof. The roofs of that day could be repaired fairly easily.

The Son of Man

Jesus called himself "the Son of Man." This expression was Jesus' favorite title for himself.

The expression "Son of Man" was used as (1) a reference to humanity in general; (2) a circumlocution for *I* as the speaker; (3) a Messianic title. In Mark, Jesus used this title most often after Peter made the Messianic confession in Mark 8:27–30. Jesus used the title as both a circumlocution for *I* and as a somewhat disguised reference to his Messianic role. In using this title Jesus could fill it with a meaning different from that of the militaristic, nationalistic messiah the Jewish people expected. Jesus was the Messiah who served and suffered on behalf of his people.

Acting on Faith

- Pray for someone who may be discouraged. Think of something proactive you can do to encourage the person.

- Think of friends who need to come to Jesus. List ways you can "bring" them closer to Jesus.

- Think of an area of your life where you have not allowed Jesus to have authority, and decide to relinquish authority to him.

Questions

1. Have you ever been in circumstances where your faith was tested and the faith of those around you helped to strengthen you and see you through?

2. Which is more important to you: that Jesus heals you physically or spiritually?

3. What obstacles did the four friends face, and how did they overcome them?

4. What are some of the obstacles you have faced in your life? How did you overcome them?

5. Who are the people you need to help by bringing them to the help Jesus provides?

6. In what ways do you need to act on your faith?

Focal Text

Mark 2:13–17,
23—3:6

Background

Mark 2:13—3:6

Main Idea

Jesus supersedes all religious and
cultural rules and traditions.

Question to Explore

To what extent are Christians
unbound from religious
and cultural rules, and
who gets to decide?

LESSON THREE

Live the Unbound Life

Study Aim

To determine principles and
implications for life today
about observing religious
and cultural rules

Study and Action Emphases

- Affirm the Bible as our authoritative guide for life and ministry
- Share the gospel with all people
- Develop a growing, vibrant faith
- Obey and serve Jesus by meeting physical, spiritual, and emotional needs

Quick Read

Responding to Jesus, the authoritative "Christ, the Son of God" (Mark 1:1), results in a life unbound from religious and cultural traditions.

My family and I recently built a house and moved in. Moving to a new house meant changing neighborhoods and, for my two youngest children, changing schools. My eldest and youngest were very excited about the move because they would be getting their own room. My middle child, however, did not like the idea of moving at all. He didn't want his own room. He liked sharing with his older brother. Too, he didn't want a new school with new friends. He liked the ones he had just fine. He didn't care that the new house was much bigger and newer. He didn't care that it was a good financial investment. In fact, he didn't care about any of the great reasons to make the move. The stack of evidence in favor of the move didn't impress him in the least. He liked things the way they were.

Change is tough. We get accustomed to the way things are. We fall into a routine (rut?) and become enamored with the traditional way of doing things. Often we cannot remember why we do certain things the way we do them. It's just the way it's always been. Challenging the status quo is a journey far away from our comfort zone and can be a dangerous and frightening endeavor.

Mark 2:13–17

13Once again Jesus went out beside the lake. A large crowd came to him, and he began to teach them. 14As he walked along, he saw Levi son of Alphaeus sitting at the tax collector's booth. "Follow me," Jesus told him, and Levi got up and followed him.

¹⁵While Jesus was having dinner at Levi's house, many tax collectors and "sinners" were eating with him and his disciples, for there were many who followed him. ¹⁶When the teachers of the law who were Pharisees saw him eating with the "sinners" and tax collectors, they asked his disciples: "Why does he eat with tax collectors and 'sinners'?"

¹⁷On hearing this, Jesus said to them, "It is not the healthy who need a doctor, but the sick. I have not come to call the righteous, but sinners."

Mark 2:23–28

²³One Sabbath Jesus was going through the grain-fields, and as his disciples walked along, they began to pick some heads of grain. ²⁴The Pharisees said to him, "Look, why are they doing what is unlawful on the Sabbath?"

²⁵He answered, "Have you never read what David did when he and his companions were hungry and in need? ²⁶In the days of Abiathar the high priest, he entered the house of God and ate the consecrated bread, which is lawful only for priests to eat. And he also gave some to his companions."

²⁷Then he said to them, "The Sabbath was made for man, not man for the Sabbath. ²⁸So the Son of Man is Lord even of the Sabbath."

Mark 3:1–6

1Another time he went into the synagogue, and a man with a shriveled hand was there. **2**Some of them were looking for a reason to accuse Jesus, so they watched him closely to see if he would heal him on the Sabbath. **3**Jesus said to the man with the shriveled hand, "Stand up in front of everyone."

4Then Jesus asked them, "Which is lawful on the Sabbath: to do good or to do evil, to save life or to kill?" But they remained silent.

5He looked around at them in anger and, deeply distressed at their stubborn hearts, said to the man, "Stretch out your hand." He stretched it out, and his hand was completely restored. **6**Then the Pharisees went out and began to plot with the Herodians how they might kill Jesus.

Challenging the Status Quo

Mark's Gospel records the amazement with which the crowds responded to Jesus' teaching. They were amazed because Jesus didn't teach as the other rabbis and religious leaders but as one who had authority. Jesus did not teach by quoting what someone else had said, but rather he stood on his own, often unique, interpretation of God's word. These unique interpretations were challenging the status quo of the religious establishment.

Last week's lesson introduced the first of a series of controversial actions in Jesus' ministry. Jesus told a paralyzed man that his sins were forgiven. The Pharisees questioned Jesus' authority to do so. In today's lesson, Jesus continued to act in such a way as to attract the suspicion and rage of the religious establishment. He was not following their traditional rules, and they confronted him at every turn.

Eating with Sinners (2:13–17)

The first confrontation came on the heels of a call to discipleship. Jesus issued the call, "Follow me," to a tax collector named Levi. Calling Levi was one of the most radical departures from tradition that Jesus could make. His association with tax collectors was enough to cast serious doubt on his authentic-ity as a teacher of Israel. Calling

Change is tough.

a tax collector to be one of his most intimate disciples was beyond comprehension. What Jesus did had to cause an immediate and sizable disturbance in every aspect of his ministry.

The Roman tax system was well-established by the first century. The Romans collected taxes from many different regions and in many different languages. Doing so was no small feat.

Their solution was to use a contract system. They divided the empire into districts and allowed local businesspeople to bid on the tax-collecting business for each district. The Romans would require a certain amount per capita. The businessperson who won the contract would be responsible for extracting, at the very least, the amount required to pay Rome. Whatever else the businessperson could force the people to pay above and beyond the Roman requirement would go into the businessperson's pockets.

Most of the tax collectors in Israel in Jesus' day were considered to have betrayed their own people, selling them out for a healthy Roman kickback. The tax collectors had isolated themselves from the general populace, who hated them. Tax collectors had justified their business and had hardened themselves to severe criticism from the religious establishment. These tax collectors were considered to be spiritually void. They were to be avoided, if at all possible.

We fall into a routine (rut?) and become enamored with the traditional way of doing things.

If a rabbi would come upon a young man who was righteous and who had followed the Mosaic law all his life, he would call him to be his disciple. This type of candidate was considered ideal for rabbinical discipleship. Calling an active tax collector to be a disciple, though, was a slap in the face of everything that was traditional. It flew in the face of every "rule" for rabbinical work. To call such a person was incomprehensible.

To make matters worse, Jesus went to Levi's home and had dinner with other tax collectors. The house of this sinner and traitor to Israel was filled with his sinful friends, who also were traitors, and Jesus was in the middle of it. So the question of the Pharisees was natural (Mark 2:16): "Why does he eat with tax collectors and 'sinners'?"

Challenging the status quo is a journey far away from our comfort zone and can be a dangerous and frightening endeavor.

Jesus defended his actions by appealing to his mission. He did not come for those who thought themselves healthy but for those who were in desperate need of a physician. These "sinners" were the very reason Jesus came to earth. Where else would Jesus be eating, if not with the very ones he came to save?

In associating with sinners, we may be going against centuries of church tradition, but we are standing in the company of Jesus. Jesus taught that leading people into a saving relationship with God was more important than the tradition of not eating with "sinners."

To Fast or Not to Fast (2:18–22)

In 2:18–22, the focus of controversy shifts from Jesus to his disciples. Of course, an attack on a rabbi's disciples was an attack on the rabbi. Jesus was asked why his disciples did not fast in the tradition of the disciples of John and the disciples of the Pharisees. The question implied that Jesus did not have the discipline among his disciples that the Pharisees and John had with theirs.

The Jewish law required fasting on only one day a year, the Day of Atonement (see Leviticus 16:29, 31; 23:27, 29, 32; Numbers 29:7[1]). As a mark of piety, however, the Pharisees fasted twice a week (Luke 18:12). Apparently, John's disciples also fasted regularly, most likely in keeping with their ascetic lifestyle (Matthew 11:18; Luke 7:33). In stark contrast, Jesus' ministry was marked with festive meals (Matt. 11:19; Luke 7:34) and fellowship with sinners (Mark 2:13–17).

> *In associating with sinners, we may be going against centuries of church tradition, but we are standing in the company of Jesus.*

Jesus responded to the question, in typical rabbinical style, with a counter question. His question used a wedding party as an analogy. *Does the wedding party mourn and grieve while the groom is with them?* The answer to the rhetorical question is obvious: *Of course not.* The presence of the groom at the wedding is reason for celebration. In the Old Testament, personal fasting (as opposed to a national fast) was most often associated with mourning, grief, or painful repentance (1 Samuel 31:13; 2 Samuel 1:12; see also Matt. 6:16). Jesus pointed out that there was no place for such expressions while the bridegroom was at the wedding. He explained that one day the bridegroom would leave the wedding and the time for fasting (accompanied by mourning) would begin.

The parable couplet of the cloth and wineskins served to emphasize Jesus' point (Mark 2:21–22). The point Jesus was making with these illustrations was that the new and the old could not coexist. John and the Pharisees represented the old covenant. Jesus represented the new. The new could not mix with the old; they were incompatible.

Jesus taught that leading people into a saving relationship with God was more important than the tradition of not eating with "sinners."

The thrust of this passage of Scripture is Christological. Just as the previous two stories, this one portrays Jesus' ministry as something new and powerful. It is the new age of salvation. The new way is evident, not only in Jesus' healing the sick (2:1–12) and eating with sinners (2:13–17) but even in the lifestyle of his disciples (celebrating instead of fasting).

In the new covenant Christ supersedes the rules and makes them serve their original purpose. This theme is amplified and made concrete in the next story, which concerns the Sabbath.

Working on the Sabbath (2:23–28)

Jesus and his disciples were walking through a grain field on the Sabbath. They plucked the seeds off the stalks of the standing grain. This was not considered stealing but was allowable according to the law (Deut. 23:25). The Pharisees' point of contention was not that the disciples were eating grain that did not belong to them but rather that they were reaping (or harvesting) on the Sabbath. This act was considered work according to most rabbinical schools.

Various rabbinical schools of thought debated the ramifications of the primary Sabbath law (Exodus 20:8–11; Deut. 5:12–15). The thrust of the debate centered on what constituted *labor* or *work*. If God instructed his people not to *work* on the Sabbath, then how would a person define *work*? The interpretations of the various laws were combined in the Mishnah, a statement of the oral traditions, which was considered binding by most rabbis. In the Mishnah,

Jesus went to the heart of God's commandments and drew from them timeless principles for living.

thirty-nine specific tasks were forbidden on the Sabbath. Reaping was one of them. The rabbis would then debate what actually constituted *reaping.* Their debates were endless.

Jesus responded to the confrontation in two ways. First he addressed the Pharisees' criticism by referring to the instance in the Old Testament when David ate the bread from the altar of the tabernacle (Mark 2:25–26; see 1 Sam. 21:1–6). Second, he dealt with the Sabbath law by placing the "Son of Man" over the "Sabbath" (Mark 2:27–28). In both instances, Jesus did not deny that he broke the Sabbath tradition by reaping. Instead, he went to the heart of the law and drew out the principle behind the law. He was not debating the scribal interpretation of the law. His argument cut to the original intent of the Sabbath law, regardless of who was interpreting it.

Jesus referenced a time when David and his men were extremely hungry from traveling. They entered the tabernacle and ate the bread because it was the only food available. Jesus pointed out that this act was illegal according to the Mosaic law, and yet David was never charged.

Jesus compared the authority of his ministry with that of Israel's greatest king. David was able to supersede the Mosaic law, in unique and dire circumstances, because he had the authority of the throne. God gave David this authority. Jesus, in the same way, had authority over the law because of the authority God had given him.

> *Living with Christ results in a life unbound from religious tradition and practice.*

In referencing David, Jesus made the issue one of authority rather than a debate over the minutia of the Sabbath law.

Jesus also placed the Sabbath in its original context, stating that the Sabbath was intended for the benefit and blessing of people, not the other way around. The traditions and interpretations of people had created an oppressive system for the observance of the Sabbath. The Sabbath laws had created a situation in which people served the Sabbath instead of the Sabbath serving people. Jesus also emphasized again his unique authority over the Sabbath laws.

THE GOSPEL OF MARK: Jesus' Works and Words

The expression "the Son of Man" carried Messianic overtones.

Healing on the Sabbath (3:1–6)

The final controversy also occurred on the Sabbath. Jesus entered a synagogue and saw a man with a withered hand. The Pharisees were watching closely to see whether Jesus would, once again, break the Old Testament law by healing on the Sabbath. Jesus knew what they were thinking and asked a question (3:4), "Which is lawful on the Sabbath: to do good or to do evil, to save life or to kill?" Jesus used the technical language of scribal legal discussions. The entire scene revolved around this question.

> *Life with Jesus is more than following a set of rules and regulations.*

As mentioned before, the religious community debated endlessly on the minutia of the law. The debate over Sabbath work laws centered on applying the law to various situations. What if a person's life was in danger on the Sabbath and only an act previously deemed as work could save the person? The Old Testament laws made certain exceptions for a case when an animal or a person might be in trouble.

Jesus was appealing to the principle behind these exceptions. His appeal was formed in two statements of comparison and contrast. Is it lawful to do good or to do evil? The answer is obvious. God's commandments are all based on doing what is good and abstaining from all that is evil. Jesus' point was that the commandment to do good was to be obeyed every day, even on the Sabbath. Jesus also asked whether it was right to kill or to save life. Again, the answer was obvious. The commandments against murder were meant for all seven days of the week. It was ridiculous to think that obeying the Sabbath law would justify allowing someone to die.

Jesus proceeded to heal the man with the withered hand, and the Pharisees could not say a word. Once again, Jesus had silenced them with an appeal to the basic principles of God's law. The Pharisees and other religious leaders began to try to find a way to destroy Jesus (3:6).

Implications and Actions

Jesus dealt with controversy over his unique teaching on a regular basis. He was attacked for his nonconformity to the traditional interpretation of the Old Testament law. He did not allow the rules and regulations mandated by the religious establishment to deter him from following the principles of his faith. Jesus went to the heart of God's commandments and drew from them timeless principles for living. He refused to bow to the human traditions surrounding God's commandments. He refused to forsake his teaching for that of the traditional established religious leadership. For this reason, they began to plot his death.

Living with Christ results in a life unbound from religious tradition and practice. Life with Jesus is more than following a set of rules and regulations. Ours is a living faith, in which we work out the implications of our salvation (see Philippians 4:12). We do this by following the principles of our faith found in God's word and by listening to God's Holy Spirit speak to our lives.

Case Study

A new family has moved into town and is visiting your church. They begin attending your Sunday School class. The husband begins to question the teacher on certain Scripture passages that pertain to the Old Testament law. After a few weeks, he seems to be steering every question back to the Old Testament law and what it forbids, according to his views. After a month, in frustration he tells the class that he just believes in reading the Bible in *black-and-white* terms, and that every Old Testament law is to be obeyed in a literal fashion. He explains that he and his family live that way and that it is the only way to be righteous and get into heaven.

How would you respond to this person? What would be the loving thing to do?

"In the Days of Abiathar"

In Mark 2:25–26 Jesus told the story of David eating the bread on the altar with an historic notation that it was "in the days of Abiathar" (Mark 2:26). This incident, however, recorded in 1 Samuel 21, occurred between David and Ahimelech, Abiathar's father. One explanation is that the Greek word *epi* can be translated *titled*, and that Jesus thus was indicating the title of the section in 1 Samuel that was titled after the more familiar Abiathar but was not referring to Abiathar himself.

Questions

1. What are some of the rules and regulations of religion that you have followed? Are they based on biblical principles?

2. What are some of the ways we adhere to tradition and perhaps fail to think about the reasons behind our actions?

3. What are the dangers of obeying rules without paying attention to God's word?

4. Is it ever "wrong" to do something good?

5. How does responding to Jesus result in a life unbound from religious and cultural traditions?

NOTES

1. "Deny yourselves" in Numbers 29:7 refers to fasting.

Showing Who Jesus Is

As we continue to move through the study of the Gospel of Mark, the section to be studied in this unit begins with Jesus departing "with his disciples to the lake" (Mark 3:7) after his initial ministry. The section extends to the midpoint of Mark's Gospel near the end of chapter 8. In this section, Jesus further established his identity as "Christ the Son of God" (1:1) by demonstrating his authority in numerous ways.

Lesson four, "More Than Meets the Eye," is on Mark 4:1–34, especially 4:21–34. In these Scriptures, Jesus clarified his identity through teaching in parables. The parables in Mark 4 teach that Jesus and his ministry were—and are—indeed "more than meets the eye."

Lesson five is a study of Jesus' victorious provision in four situations that seemed hopeless—a storm at sea; a demon-possessed man who was too violent to live in his community; a young girl who was deathly ill and who then died; a woman who had been ill for years, unable to get well. The lesson, titled "Jesus and Hopeless Situations," is a study of Mark 4:35—5:43.

Lesson six, on Mark 7:1–23, "When Cleanliness Is Not Next to Godliness," contrasts the approach of Jesus to that of the Pharisees. It emphasizes that, as the Main Idea states, "True goodness—and evil—come from within and not from keeping the norms of tradition and culture, even Christian tradition and culture."

Lesson seven, "There Are None So Blind," is on Mark 8:11–26, and calls for seeing truly who Jesus is and responding to him.[1]

UNIT TWO. SHOWING WHO JESUS IS

Lesson 4	More Than Meets the Eye	Mark 4:21–34
Lesson 5	Jesus and Hopeless Situations	Mark 4:35—5:43
Lesson 6	When Cleanliness Is Not Next to Godliness	Mark 7:1–23
Lesson 7	There Are None So Blind	Mark 8:11–26

NOTES

1. Unless otherwise indicated, all Scripture quotations are from the New International Version.

Main Idea

Who Jesus is and what the results of his ministry are and will be are more, much more, than meets the eye.

Question to Explore

When worldly power and methods seem so often to be what works and prevails, does it make sense to stake our hopes and futures on Jesus and his way?

LESSON FOUR

More Than Meets the Eye

Study Aim

To identify implications of these parables for Jesus' work, our church, and my life

Study and Action Emphases

- Affirm the Bible as our authoritative guide for life and ministry
- Share the gospel with all people
- Develop a growing, vibrant faith
- Include all God's family in decision-making and service
- Equip people for servant leadership

Quick Read

Through three simple parables Jesus painted a picture of his identity and the endless possibilities that await his closest followers.

I had worn glasses since the fourth grade, and now I was nineteen. I had been legally blind for years. My vision had deteriorated to 20/1600 in my "good eye." My "bad eye" was 20/2000. In layman's terms, I never saw the ocean until I was submerged. I took a telescope to the ball game, and my seat was on the front row. I typed in a large font—48. Then Russian ophthalmologists introduced something called radial keratotomy (RK).

So I went under the knife. No, this wasn't the pain-free, drive-through lasik surgery of today. They used a knife. I felt all sixteen cuts in each eye. After the surgery I couldn't see a thing. My world had gone from blurry to black. Then they removed the patches.

Now, I didn't just see trees. I saw leaves. People with 20/2000 vision see just as much as 20/20 people. They just don't see it clearly.

Let's take a walk in God's forest. If you want to see leaves and see them clearly, you'll need the help of the Great Ophthalmologist. We must draw close enough for him to change our vision. In the three parables before us, we will discover possibilities that are more than meet the eye.

Mark 4:21–34

21He said to them, "Do you bring in a lamp to put it under a bowl or a bed? Instead, don't you put it on its stand? **22**For whatever is hidden is meant to be disclosed, and whatever is concealed is meant to be brought out into the open. **23**If anyone has ears to hear, let him hear."

24"Consider carefully what you hear," he continued. "With the measure you use, it will be measured to you—and even more. **25**Whoever has will be given more; whoever does not have, even what he has will be taken from him."

26He also said, "This is what the kingdom of God is like. A man scatters seed on the ground. **27**Night and day, whether he sleeps or gets up, the seed sprouts and grows, though he does not know how. **28**All by itself the soil produces grain—first the stalk, then the head, then the full kernel in the head. **29**As soon as the grain is ripe, he puts the sickle to it, because the harvest has come."

30Again he said, "What shall we say the kingdom of God is like, or what parable shall we use to describe it? **31**It is like a mustard seed, which is the smallest seed you plant in the ground. **32**Yet when planted, it grows and becomes the largest of all garden plants, with such big branches that the birds of the air can perch in its shade."

33With many similar parables Jesus spoke the word to them, as much as they could understand. **34**He did not say anything to them without using a parable. But when he was alone with his own disciples, he explained everything.

The Parable of the Lamp (4:21–25)

On the heels of one of Jesus' most quoted stories, the parable of the four soils (Mark 4:1–20), he taught his followers a lesson about purpose. The lamp was a small clay bowl or saucer. It was a fixture in every home. The bowl was made with a spout to hold a wick. It contained a few ounces of oil, serving as fuel. The lamp stood on a shelf, centrally placed in the house.

The lamp existed to produce light, for three purposes. First, the light served as a guide. Second, the light removed the darkness in the house. Third, the light exposed that which was hidden. The "hidden" would be "disclosed," while the "concealed is meant to be brought out into the open" (4:22). We all look good in a mirror, at least until the light comes on!

. . . Great movements have small beginnings.

I live in an old house, in an old neighborhood, with lots of old furniture. I love antiques. Unfortunately, old stuff wears out. We have a beautiful, antique lamp in our living room. The lamp has just one problem. It no longer works. The old lamp still looks great, but that is not the purpose of a lamp. It was created to produce light. We were not created to look good (welcome news for some of us). We were created to put off light.

Jesus said to watch out for bowls and beds. Bowls hide the light. Beds—perhaps mats on the floor—smother the light. We are challenged by many bowls and beds, such as compromise, complacency, and carnality. They all seek to snuff out our flame.

Before moving on to the next parable, Jesus offered the lone command of our text. We are told to hear what he says (4:23). The word "hear" means to listen with intensity and understanding. Then the Master offered a promise and a warning. God blesses us based on our service. We receive, we respond, and then we receive "even more" (4:24). The key is not how much we have but what we do with it. For those who are disobedient, there will be a great loss. Jesus spoke in accounting terms. People who are disobedient will run a deficit.

The Parable of the Seed (4:26–29)

This parable is unique to Mark's writings. Jesus told the story of scattered seed becoming a great harvest. Jesus began his series of parables with a discourse on four soils (4:1–20). He concluded with two stories about the *right* soil. The seed represents the word of God. The harvest may represent the kingdom at large, or God's work in each of his children. Jesus revealed three steps to the harvesting of the fruit. These steps could be stated, *Sow, grow, and mow.* Our job is to scatter the seed. God provides the harvest, which becomes a point of celebration for his children.

The process begins with faithful sowing. Notice, nothing is said about the amount of seed scattered.

Our job is simply to scatter as much seed as we have. God will take care of the results. Healthy seed planted in the right soil produces fruit. We are to be faithful sowers.

The next step is patient waiting. "Night and day, whether he sleeps or gets up, the seed sprouts and grows, though he does not know how" (4:27). God does more while we sleep than we can do awake! Growth occurs in the dark, as the handiwork of God. Only God can produce growth in the believer and in his kingdom. Bible study is critical, as is prayer, but Bible study and prayer only *prepare* us for growth. Real maturation is brought about where no eye can see, by the hand of God himself. Our family recently returned from a vacation in New York. We came home to taller grass in our yard than we found in all of Manhattan. I had spread the fertilizer, and then I waited. God took care of the rest.

God requires our best effort, but the real energy, growth, and progress can be attributed only to the hidden work of God.

The final step in the process is joyful reaping. The soil produces fruit "all by itself" (4:28). There exists a secret relationship of seeds and soil. The promise is fruit. This short story tells us two things. We are to be involved in the work of the kingdom. We plant seeds. Then, God is responsible for the increase. The sower takes his or her sickle, a curved blade mounted in a short handle, and harvests the crop he did not produce.

The Parable of the Mustard Seed (4:30–32)

Jesus concluded his series of kingdom lessons with a short talk about a small seed that produced great results. This final parable has fewer than sixty-five words and can be quoted in about fifteen seconds. The average sermon is a hundred times longer (twenty-five minutes) but says a hundred times less!

The story is about a mustard plant, used for three purposes. The leaves were a common vegetable, and the seeds were enjoyed as a condiment and for medicinal purposes. The mustard seed is the size of a pinhead. Twenty thousand seeds weigh one ounce. So the smallest seed in Palestine produced the largest shrub in Palestine, sometimes reaching heights of ten to fifteen feet. Jesus said this "garden plant" would produce "such big branches that the birds of the air can perch in its shade" (4:32). The growth also provided comforting shelter for weary travelers.

Jesus spoke the language of the day, and so must we.

Allegory lovers cherish the parable of the mustard seed. Theories of deep, hidden meanings abound. To some, the birds represent Gentiles. The branches are churches. The small seed represents a short, brief word in one's youth. The shade is a reprieve from the storms of life. So people who see allegorical meanings in parables suggest.

Biblical interpretation is not an exact science, of course. But our task is not to bog down in such a manner in what is trivial and subjective, but to apply the principles that are unmistakable. Three clear principles emerge from the text.

First, great movements have small beginnings. Scholars interpret the passage to represent growth in the Christian, the church, the kingdom, or all three. Indeed, the growth of this movement called Christianity was about to sweep the known world. We see the explosion of mustard seeds all around us and in our churches today. A mustard seed may be a new convert, a young child, or a fresh idea. My brother, Dr. Jim Denison, is pastor of Park Cities Baptist Church in Dallas, Texas. He and I were a couple of mustard seeds who rode a bus to church more than thirty years ago, only to become pastors and seed-planters ourselves.

Our job is not to be brilliant but to walk near the Master.

The mustard seed carries a second principle. Jesus said, "When planted, it grows" (4:32). Our job is to plant; it is God's job to provide the increase. Each of us has the same calling as Christians. God requires our best effort, but the real energy, growth, and progress can be attributed only to the hidden work of God. This is a consistent theme of many of the New Testament parables.

A third principle is that we, like the mustard plant, exist to meet the needs of others. The mustard seed affects many people. Vegetables, seasoning, shelter, and medication are all products of a tiny seed in the right soil. Every believer is called and equipped to be a part of the body of Christ. In the church, "God has combined the members of the body" (1 Corinthians 12:24) to do a work far greater than any individual seed. The key is not the size of the seed but the soil in which it is planted.

The Best Way to Teach (4:33–34)

These verses may provide the greatest seminary instruction ever offered on the principles of teaching and proclamation. Two aspects must always be in place: the right message and the right method. The message is, of course, the gospel, or good news. That never changes. Methods must adapt to the audience, though. Paul said,

> *We are to be lamps, offering guidance and direction to a dark world.*

"I have become all things to all men so that by all possible means I might save some" (1 Cor. 9:22). Jesus spoke the language of the day, and so must we. As we zoom in close and join the conversation, we learn four principles to the teaching method.

First, Jesus told stories. "He did not say anything to them without using a parable" (4:34). Verse 33 suggests that Jesus told stories beyond those recorded in Scripture. "With many similar parables Jesus spoke the word to them . . ." (4:33). Teachers need to hear Jesus' message, but also they need to pay attention to his method. We must learn to tell stories. People will forget Sunday morning's masterfully crafted sermon outline by halftime of the afternoon football game. But they will remember stories for years.

Second, our Lord spoke to the crowds. His passion was to win the world. The four Gospels contain many references to Jesus ministering to the "crowds" or "multitudes." While Jesus spent great periods of time with the Twelve, he was often criticized by the spiritually elite because he spent a lot of time with the "wrong crowd."

Third, we see the central plan in the Master's teaching. He spoke in a way that could be understood. Jesus taught "as much as they could understand" (4:33). He sought to influence, not impress. The sign of good teaching is not an audience responding, *That is deep.* A better response would be, *I see it, I know what to do, and I'll do it.* Most of Jesus' words had to do with application. When I prepare any message, I always keep in mind one question: *So what?* If a message cannot answer the *so what* question, it does not need to be delivered.

We must also look for mustard seed opportunities to plant ministries that can bear amazing fruit.

The fourth step in Jesus' method was to pull his inner circle aside for further explanation. "When he was alone with his own disciples, he explained everything" (4:34). The word for "explained" is a continuous action verb. Jesus *kept on explaining* his stories.

Good teachers are always looking for strong disciples whom they can pull out of the crowd for personal instruction. A timeless truth is that those closest to the Master understand his message. The call of the believer is not to be brilliant. His or her call is to walk close enough to the Savior that he or she can hear and understand the Savior's voice.

We are to spread the seed of God's word.

Implications and Actions

Jesus taught his followers through stories. Our job is not to be brilliant but to walk near the Master. His voice is clear. We are to be lamps, offering guidance and direction to a dark world. We are to spread the seed of God's word. We must also look for mustard seed opportunities to plant ministries that can bear amazing fruit.

Mustard Seeds of Yesterday

God has always planted mustard seeds. Our Christian heritage has planted shade trees we enjoy today. Here are a few examples. Probably you can think of others.

- *Sunday School.* Robert Raikes (1735–1811), a newspaper publisher in England, was devoted to prison reform. His interest moved to preventing crime among poor children. Because the children worked during the week, Raikes offered a Sunday School, beginning in 1780. The children came to study the Scriptures. Millions of people of all ages have been part of Sunday School classes through the years.

- *Reformation.* The Reformation movement was precipitated most famously by Martin Luther's Ninety-Five Theses, nailed to the door of the church on October 31, 1517.

- *Salvation Army.* William Booth founded the "Christian Mission" in 1865, in London. Later changed to "Salvation Army" because it was organized as an army, with officers, the organization spread to America in 1880. Millions have been blessed because of this benevolent dream of Mr. Booth.

Bringing It Home

- List two or three opportunities in your regular schedule where you can shine your lamp.

- Look for places to scatter the seed of God's word, and trust God for the results.

- Ask God for a fresh dream of a mustard plant in your future.

- Keep the mustard seed in mind when you become discouraged.

Questions

1. Reflecting on the parable of the lamp, what threatens to darken your light?

2. Can you think of any mustard seed opportunities God may be placing on the horizon for your church?

3. In what ways could you encourage your pastor or Sunday School teacher in teaching God's word?

4. How do you think the work of Christ might be more than meets the eye today?

Main Idea

Jesus specializes in helping people in situations that seem hopeless.

Question to Explore

What can we do when the situation seems hopeless?

LESSON FIVE

Jesus and Hopeless Situations

Study Aim

To identify the common elements in the events of this passage and state implications for my life of what Jesus did in each

Study and Action Emphases

- Affirm the Bible as our authoritative guide for life and ministry
- Share the gospel with all people
- Develop a growing, vibrant faith
- Include all God's family in decision-making and service
- Value all people as created in the image of God
- Encourage healthy families
- Obey and serve Jesus by meeting physical, spiritual, and emotional needs

Quick Read

Storms come in many forms, and they affect everybody. Through four hopeless situations Jesus presented himself as the answer to every crisis and the comfort in every storm.

It was 7:30 A.M. She was an uninvited guest, and we would not forget her. Her name was Alicia. Her full name was Hurricane Alicia, and she brought our Gulf Coast area ten inches of rain and winds of 115 miles per hour.

Many times I have been the token dummy interviewed on TV, coming in from the water during tropical storms and "small" hurricanes. But Alicia was different. I was overmatched, and I knew not to test the fierceness of her winds and waves.

We all face storms in life. When they get rough, we need help. That is when the Peacemaker steps in. In the passage before us, we see four examples of the most vicious storms that can rock a person's life. This is not a lesson about God protecting us *from* the storm but God about protecting us *in* the storm. Whether you are entering a storm, in a storm, or coming out of one, the God of the storm offers to be your raft and protector.

Mark 4:35–41

35That day when evening came, he said to his disciples, "Let us go over to the other side." 36Leaving the crowd behind, they took him along, just as he was, in the boat. There were also other boats with him. 37A furious squall came up, and the waves broke over the boat, so that it was nearly swamped. 38Jesus was in the stern, sleeping on a cushion. The disciples woke him and said to him, "Teacher, don't you care if we drown?"

39He got up, rebuked the wind and said to the waves, "Quiet! Be still!" Then the wind died down and it was completely calm.

40He said to his disciples, "Why are you so afraid? Do you still have no faith?"

41They were terrified and asked each other, "Who is this? Even the wind and the waves obey him!"

Mark 5:1–43

1They went across the lake to the region of the Gerasenes. **2**When Jesus got out of the boat, a man with an evil spirit came from the tombs to meet him. **3**This man lived in the tombs, and no one could bind him any more, not even with a chain. **4**For he had often been chained hand and foot, but he tore the chains apart and broke the irons on his feet. No one was strong enough to subdue him. **5**Night and day among the tombs and in the hills he would cry out and cut himself with stones.

6When he saw Jesus from a distance, he ran and fell on his knees in front of him. **7**He shouted at the top of his voice, "What do you want with me, Jesus, Son of the Most High God? Swear to God that you won't torture me!" **8**For Jesus had said to him, "Come out of this man, you evil spirit!"

9Then Jesus asked him, "What is your name?"

"My name is Legion," he replied, "for we are many." [10]And he begged Jesus again and again not to send them out of the area.

[11]A large herd of pigs was feeding on the nearby hillside. [12]The demons begged Jesus, "Send us among the pigs; allow us to go into them." [13]He gave them permission, and the evil spirits came out and went into the pigs. The herd, about two thousand in number, rushed down the steep bank into the lake and were drowned.

[14]Those tending the pigs ran off and reported this in the town and countryside, and the people went out to see what had happened. [15]When they came to Jesus, they saw the man who had been possessed by the legion of demons, sitting there, dressed and in his right mind; and they were afraid. [16]Those who had seen it told the people what had happened to the demon-possessed man—and told about the pigs as well. [17]Then the people began to plead with Jesus to leave their region.

[18]As Jesus was getting into the boat, the man who had been demon-possessed begged to go with him. [19]Jesus did not let him, but said, "Go home to your family and tell them how much the Lord has done for you, and how he has had mercy on you." [20]So the man went away and began to tell in the Decapolis how much Jesus had done for him. And all the people were amazed.

[21]When Jesus had again crossed over by boat to the other side of the lake, a large crowd gathered around him while he was by the lake. [22]Then one of the synagogue rulers, named Jairus, came there. Seeing Jesus, he fell at his feet [23]and pleaded earnestly with him, "My

little daughter is dying. Please come and put your hands on her so that she will be healed and live." **24**So Jesus went with him.

A large crowd followed and pressed around him. **25**And a woman was there who had been subject to bleeding for twelve years. **26**She had suffered a great deal under the care of many doctors and had spent all she had, yet instead of getting better she grew worse. **27**When she heard about Jesus, she came up behind him in the crowd and touched his cloak, **28**because she thought, "If I just touch his clothes, I will be healed." **29**Immediately her bleeding stopped and she felt in her body that she was freed from her suffering.

30At once Jesus realized that power had gone out from him. He turned around in the crowd and asked, "Who touched my clothes?"

31"You see the people crowding against you," his disciples answered, "and yet you can ask, 'Who touched me?'"

32But Jesus kept looking around to see who had done it. **33**Then the woman, knowing what had happened to her, came and fell at his feet and, trembling with fear, told him the whole truth. **34**He said to her, "Daughter, your faith has healed you. Go in peace and be freed from your suffering."

35While Jesus was still speaking, some men came from the house of Jairus, the synagogue ruler. "Your daughter is dead," they said. "Why bother the teacher any more?"

36Ignoring what they said, Jesus told the synagogue ruler, "Don't be afraid; just believe."

37He did not let anyone follow him except Peter, James and John the brother of James. **38**When they came to the home of the synagogue ruler, Jesus saw a commotion, with people crying and wailing loudly. **39**He went in and said to them, "Why all this commotion and wailing? The child is not dead but asleep." **40**But they laughed at him.

After he put them all out, he took the child's father and mother and the disciples who were with him, and went in where the child was. **41**He took her by the hand and said to her, "Talitha koum!" (which means, "Little girl, I say to you, get up!"). **42**Immediately the girl stood up and walked around (she was twelve years old). At this they were completely astonished. **43**He gave strict orders not to let anyone know about this, and told them to give her something to eat.

The Perfect Storm (4:35–41)

Jesus had just taught the great parables of the soils, lamp, seed, and mustard plant. He then led the disciples to the east side of the lake. Jesus knew the storm was coming, but he went anyway. He is never caught off guard by life's storms. Modern preaching often promises an escape from storms, while Christ often leads us *into* the storms. Notice in this incident a paradox of life. When we take control, God rests; when we rest, God can take control.

Jesus pulled away from the crowd, as we all must do at times (Mark 4:36). The sudden storm was typical for the Sea of Galilee, nestled between mountains, almost 700 feet below sea level. Jesus was at the stern of the boat. Exhausted from his teaching ministry, Jesus was asleep, unaffected by the storm. Neither the rocking of the boat nor the spray in his face could awaken the Master.

We all face storms in life. When they get rough, we need help.

awaken the Master. This elicited an obvious response from the disciples (4:38): "Don't you care?" The disciples responded in fear rather than faith. They had seen miracles, but they panicked in the storm.

Jesus responded with a simple command: "Quiet! Be still!" (4:39). This brought an immediate calm. The seas and wind were out of control, but not Jesus.

Just as the disciples chose their response ("afraid" means *cowardly fear*), we choose how we respond to life's storms. The disciples asked, "Who is this?" They still did not understand.

When Mark wrote this account, Roman persecution had already begun. But for the hopeless, there is hope.

The Crazed Demoniac (5:1–20)

The storm now behind him, Jesus arrived at the east side of the lake. What followed would have lasting impact on world evangelism and the strategy of missions. Jesus did not cross over the lake and endure the storm to win just one man's soul. The area on the east side of the lake was predominantly Gentile. His visit there thus suggests Jesus' concern for the whole world, Gentiles as well as Jews. To the Savior, this one crazed lunatic was worth saving, but, as we saw in last week's lesson, there is more than meets the eye.

This is not a lesson about God protecting us from the storm but God about protecting us in the storm.

Mark and Luke speak of one demoniac, while Matthew says there were two (Matthew 8:28–34; Luke 8:26–39). There need be no contradiction. Neither Mark nor Luke say there was *only* one; their focus may have been on the more prominent demoniac who did all the speaking. This amazing story took place in "the region of the Gerasenes" (Mark 5:1), an area dominated by Gentiles. This explains the herd of pigs (5:11), considered unclean by the Jews (Leviticus 11:7–8). The man called Legion (Mark 5:9) came "from the tombs to meet *him*" (5:2, italics added for emphasis). Jesus was with the Twelve, but Legion came out to meet only *him*—Jesus. The tombs were burial caves carved from rocky hillsides, accommodating both the dead and the alive, like Legion.

The spiritual encounter that followed was of historic proportion. This was not the disciples' first demonic battle (see 1:23–27), but the magnitude of this event would be unequaled in their early ministry.

Legion would be considered unclean on three levels. He was a Gentile, was possessed by demons, and lived among the tombs. No one was able to "subdue" him (5:4). "Subdue" conveyed the image of taming a wild animal. He cried out and cut himself with sharp rocks (5:5). This man was a truly frightening creature.

Legion's reaction to the sight of Jesus was immediate and startling. He ran toward Christ and then "fell on his knees in front of him" (5:6). This act was an acknowledgement of superior power. Demons, even by the thousands, cannot stand up to the power of God. Then the demons spoke (5:7): "What do you want with me?" The message was really, *Would you just leave me alone?* Jesus would not, for the soul of one person was simply too valuable. The precise words of Legion carried a lesson of their own. Legion called Jesus

The disciples responded in fear rather than faith.

"Son of the Most High God" (5:7). The religious elite of the Jews were blind, but the demons *got it*.

Jesus' actions were quick and clear. Expelling the demons would require no theatrical performance. He spoke just eight words. "Come out of this man, you evil spirit" (5:8). Jesus then asked, "What is your name?" (5:9). In the understatement of the story, the spirit spokesman said, "My name is Legion . . . for we are *many*" (5:9, italics added for emphasis). "Legion" was a Latin term for a Roman military unit of from 4,000 to 6,000 men. By "many," Legion meant, *There are 6,000 of us and only one of you, and yet we are outnumbered.* The demons could muster no defense but rather only a weak response. Legion "begged Jesus again and again" to allow the demons to remain in the area (5:10). The demons hoped for the opportunity to continue their torturous ways.

> *We never find ourselves in a place of hopelessness that lies beyond Jesus' reach.*

Part two of the story was even more bizarre. "A large herd of pigs was feeding on the nearby hillside" (5:11). Until now, only one demon spoke (5:10). Now, they all spoke (5:12). Their plea was rather odd. They continued to beg, now to be cast into the pigs. This was their idea! Why would 6,000 demons want to live in 2,000 pigs? The Bible does not say. But clearly, the demons would rather destroy pigs than do nothing. Jesus "gave them permission" (5:13). Remember, Satan cannot do anything to harm us, without God's permission. So the man was saved at the expense of 2,000 pigs. One person is worth that, and more, to God.

The response to this miracle was immediate. First, those assigned to caring for the pigs reacted. They told the story to those in the nearby town and countryside (5:14). The second response came from those who heard the incredible account. They "went out to see what had happened" (5:14). They saw Jesus, and then they saw "the man who had been possessed" (5:15). What they saw was a former crazed and dangerous man now sitting calmly, properly dressed, and of sound mind. They could have responded with joy to be with the Healer, with gratitude for the healing, and with thanksgiving that they would no longer live under the threat of this wild man from the tombs. Instead, "they were afraid" (5:15). They preferred a problem they were familiar with over a solution they did not understand.

The third response came from the neighbors. Those hearing from these eyewitnesses begged to be left alone, just as the demons had pleaded (5:17). They had just heard and seen incredible news. The headline in the *Decapolis Daily News* might have read, *Legion Healed! Healer Asked to Leave Town!* As with today, even the best news of the movement of God was not widely embraced.

The fourth response came from Jesus. He left, at their request (5:18). Then we witness the response of the man who had been known as Legion. He, too, begged for something. In a great paradox, when the demons begged, Jesus granted their request (5:10). Too, Jesus granted the request of the masses (5:17). But when the convert

. . . For the hopeless, there is hope.

begged for more time with Jesus, Jesus denied his plea. Jesus stuck with his plan for coming across the lake in the first place. This is a story about hope, not only for one man who lived in the cemetery but also for the thousands who lived in the Decapolis (Greek, *ten cities*), a mainly Gentile area. Jesus sent the man off as the first missionary to the Gentiles, equipped with a

THE GOSPEL OF MARK: *Jesus' Works and Words*

changed life and a personal testimony. Legion had his life back. Then, in the final response to the miracle, "all the people were amazed" (5:20). For the hopeless, there is hope.

A Dead Girl and Sick Woman (5:21–43)

Jesus endured a storm, a trip across a lake, and 6,000 demons in order to spread hope. Not surprisingly, another large crowd greeted Jesus on his return.

Always willing to meet the individual within the crowd, Jesus responded to a man named Jairus, a synagogue ruler. His duties included looking after the synagogue building, performing administrative tasks, and distributing alms. He surely knew of Jesus' reputation from Jesus' prior ministry in Capernaum. Jairus's daughter was critically ill, too sick to be brought to the Master. The bereaved father "fell at his feet" and begged Jesus to go to his daughter (5:22–23).

They preferred a problem they were familiar with over a solution they did not understand.

Jesus could have healed the girl with a simple blessing, spoken at that moment from afar, as he did for the centurion's servant (Luke 7:7). If Jairus had possessed a stronger faith, perhaps he would have asked for such a healing. The good news is that Jesus responds to faith, as weak and undeveloped as it might be. Rather than condemn the man's incomplete faith,

"Jesus went with him" (Mark 5:24), and the crowd followed.

Once again, Jesus took time for the individual. Another person was in the crowd following Jesus. A woman "who had been subject to bleeding for twelve years" (5:25) had lost all hope. She had tried every doctor and spent all she had, but she had only gotten worse. The "bleeding" would have made her to be considered *unclean*, unable to go to the synagogue or maintain normal social relationships.

Perhaps to avoid making Jesus unclean, she touched only his robe. She was immediately restored. The response of the Master revealed his real mission. "Who touched my clothes?" he asked (5:30). He wanted not only to heal her, but also to establish a personal relationship. In declaring her "healed" (5:34), Jesus

For those who seem to be without hope, there is hope.

used a word that often is translated *saved*. Then Jesus told her to "go in peace" (5:34). A literal rendering of the text would read, "Go *into* peace." Jesus sent her off to a life of lasting peace.

By now, Jairus must have been exasperated at the delay. Then he heard the words with which no parent is equipped to deal. "Your daughter is dead" (5:35). Before Jairus could speak, Jesus encouraged him to act out of faith rather than fear. "Just believe," Jesus said (5:36). The word "believe" means *keep on believing*.

Then the Lord created an inner circle of Peter, James, and John, and allowed them to experience things others could not (5:37). Upon his arrival at the house, Jesus excluded a second group. Those who responded negatively to his promise of healing were not allowed to see the miracle (5:38–39).

Jesus and the three disciples were greeted by professional mourners, a common practice of the day. Jesus said the girl was "not dead but asleep" (5:39). "They laughed at him" (5:40). Their laughter would become their judgment. To the crowd, the problem was permanent. To the Giver of hope, the problem was temporary. Jesus took the girl's hand and told her to rise. Touching the dead girl would render Jesus unclean in the eyes of the Old Testament law. The girl was raised up, not in the sick condition that led to her death, but able to walk around (5:42). This restoration to life would join those of Lazarus (John 11:1–44) and the boy near the village of Nain (Luke 7:11–15).

Our task is to react out of our faith rather than our fears.

Then Jesus gave odd instructions. He had sent Legion off to spread the word to ten cities, but here "he gave strict orders not to let anyone know about this" (Mark 5:43). Why the secrecy? Jesus knew what would happen if the word got out too fast. His opposition would be stirred before his time had come to die. Also, the focus would be on the miracles instead of on the message.

Jesus' final words are fascinating. He "told them to give her something to eat" (5:43). He cared about the girl, but an additional meaning is that the parents still had work to do in the aftermath of the miracle. He left the parents with a timeless principle. Every blessing and every miracle generates new responsibilities. One theme is clear, from the perfect storm, the crazed demoniac, the healing of the woman, and the restoration of the girl. For those who seem to be without hope, there is hope.

Implications and Actions

We live in a world in desperate need of hope. Jesus spread hope wherever he went. He joins people in their most desperate hours: a great storm, demonic warfare, illness, and even death. We never find ourselves in a place of hopelessness that lies beyond Jesus' reach. Our task is to react out of our faith rather than our fears.

All People Count

Throughout the Gospel of Mark we are discovering a Savior who cares equally for all people. Your church should adopt this same passion. Here are a few examples of the diversity of people who matter to God, found in the Book of Mark.

- The person who was paralyzed (2:1–12)

- The person with an evil spirit (5:1–20)

- A religious leader (5:22)

- A sick woman (5:25–34)

- A twelve-year-old girl (5:41–42)

- A woman from a foreign land (7:25–30)

- Children (10:13–16)

- A wealthy person (10:17–23)

- A blind beggar (10:46–52)

- Jewish political and religious leaders (12:13–27)

- A Roman governor (15:1–15)

Bringing It Home

- Define your current storm. List ways you can respond by faith.

- Ask God to direct you to a "Legion," who can affect many upon his or her conversion.

- Think of someone in the crowd who needs to touch the Master.

- Pray for the opportunity to join a small group (Peter, James, and John) who can walk together with the Savior.

Questions

1. Jesus often pulled away from the crowd. Why do you think Jesus did this? When can you plan to get away from the crowd?

2. When you face turbulence and storms, do you generally respond out of faith or out of fear?

3. The people of Decapolis were "amazed" at the changes in Legion's life. In what ways has God made amazing changes in your life and in your church?

4. The woman touched Jesus (his clothes). She was healed, and Jesus began a relationship with her. In what ways could your Sunday School class help people touch the Lord?

Main Idea

True goodness—and evil—come from within and not from keeping the norms of tradition and culture, even Christian tradition and culture.

Question to Explore

How can we keep faith from hardening into mere tradition?

LESSON SIX

When Cleanliness Is Not Next to Godliness

Study Aim

To contrast the approach of Jesus and the Pharisees and to identify implications for being a person of genuine faith

Study and Action Emphases

- Affirm the Bible as our authoritative guide for life and ministry
- Develop a growing, vibrant faith
- Value all people as created in the image of God
- Equip people for servant leadership

Quick Read

The Pharisees accused the disciples of ignoring the oral traditions they had treasured for centuries. Jesus responded by declaring that the source of both good and evil is the human heart.

As a boy, I think I heard all the great proverbs. I thought they were surely *Proverbs*, as from the Book of Proverbs. "Don't swim until an hour after you eat, or you'll get a cramp." "Birds of a feather flock together." "All good boys eat spinach." "God helps those who help themselves." Maybe the best known proverb was, "Cleanliness is next to godliness."

That is a proverb with a small *p*. But I remember that old proverb well. Later, as a student of Scripture, I learned that the idea behind this proverb might well go back at least 2,000 years. The well-educated Pharisees embraced the oral tradition that suggested it was sinful (not merely poor manners) for people to eat without first washing their hands in a carefully pre-scribed fashion.

Jesus responded to the legalism and hypocrisy of the Pharisees with pointed criticism and insight. He declared the true source of evil and good. He attacked empty, vain worship and evil actions and attitudes. The theme of Mark 7 is that true godliness is a matter of the heart, not mere outward expression. The question for you, your class, and your church is the Question to Explore: *How can we keep our faith from hardening into mere tradition?*

Mark 7:1–23

¹The Pharisees and some of the teachers of the law who had come from Jerusalem gathered around Jesus and

2saw some of his disciples eating food with hands that were "unclean," that is, unwashed. **3**(The Pharisees and all the Jews do not eat unless they give their hands a ceremonial washing, holding to the tradition of the elders. **4**When they come from the marketplace they do not eat unless they wash. And they observe many other traditions, such as the washing of cups, pitchers and kettles.)

5So the Pharisees and teachers of the law asked Jesus, "Why don't your disciples live according to the tradition of the elders instead of eating their food with 'unclean' hands?"

6He replied, "Isaiah was right when he prophesied about you hypocrites; as it is written:

"'These people honor me with their lips,
but their hearts are far from me.
7 They worship me in vain;
their teachings are but rules taught by men.'

8You have let go of the commands of God and are holding on to the traditions of men."

9And he said to them: "You have a fine way of setting aside the commands of God in order to observe your own traditions! **10**For Moses said, 'Honor your father and your mother,' and, 'Anyone who curses his father or mother must be put to death.' **11**But you say that if a man says to his father or mother: 'Whatever help you might otherwise have received from me is Corban' (that is, a gift devoted to God), **12**then you no longer let him do anything for his father or mother. **13**Thus you nullify the word of God by your tradition that you have handed down. And you do many things like that."

14Again Jesus called the crowd to him and said, "Listen to me, everyone, and understand this. **15**Nothing outside a man can make him 'unclean' by going into him. Rather, it is what comes out of a man that makes him 'unclean.'"

17After he had left the crowd and entered the house, his disciples asked him about this parable. **18**"Are you so dull?" he asked. "Don't you see that nothing that enters a man from the outside can make him 'unclean'? **19**For it doesn't go into his heart but into his stomach, and then out of his body." (In saying this, Jesus declared all foods "clean.")

20He went on: "What comes out of a man is what makes him 'unclean.' **21**For from within, out of men's hearts, come evil thoughts, sexual immorality, theft, murder, adultery, **22**greed, malice, deceit, lewdness, envy, slander, arrogance and folly. **23**All these evils come from inside and make a man 'unclean.'"

The Situation Room (7:1–4)

In the previous study, Jesus and three of his disciples were in the home of a synagogue ruler, whose daughter was raised from the dead (Mark 5:37–42). Mark 6 pictures Jesus being rejected at his hometown, Nazareth (6:1–6a); sending out the Twelve (6:6b–13); feeding 5,000 men (6:32–44); and walking on the stormy sea (6:45–56). Then the religious leaders "gathered around Jesus" (7:1). Our Lord seemed always to draw a crowd.

The Pharisees advocated minute obedience to Jewish law and traditions. "Teachers of the law" (7:1) were professional interpreters of the law, also called "scribes" (NRSV, NASB).

Together, the Pharisees and teachers of the law "noticed his disciples" (7:2). The disciples were eating a meal without first washing their hands. These religious leaders considered this omission by the disciples to be unfathomably wrong. The disciples, though, were not in violation of the Old Testament law, as represented primarily by the Ten Commandments and also by the first five Old Testament books.

They reduced spirituality to legalism and procedure.

Mark's audience needed explanation, which Mark gave them. This ceremonial hand-washing was said to cleanse people who might have become "unclean" without knowing it. The washing can be seen in the ceremonies of the ancient Hebrew tabernacle, in which priests washed their hands and feet before performing sacred duties (Exodus 30:17–21). Oral law expanded this practice to include all Jews, to be practiced before formal prayers and later before meals.

The Pharisees' concern was one of appearance, not hygiene. They reduced spirituality to legalism and procedure. They seemed to think that if they lived perfectly they would gain the respect of God.

These legalists practiced "many other traditions" (Mark 7:4). Scholars number these "many" traditions in the thousands.

In this instance, Jews who had walked among people in "the marketplace" were obligated to undergo this ceremonial washing of their hands (7:4). This act signified being cleansed from the uncleanness of the people with whom they came in contact. Oral tradition dictated that one's hands had to be free of any sand or gravel. The water for this washing was kept in a special large stone jar, to keep the water clean. Hands were to be held out with fingertips up. Water was poured over

Unfortunately, many continue to embrace traditions over God's word.

the hands, and it ran down to the wrists. With hands still wet, each hand was rubbed by the opposite fist. Then, with fingers pointed down, water was poured out, starting at the wrists. The water would run off the fingertips. To the Pharisees and scribes, this was religion.

The Dueling Dialogue (7:5–19)

The Pharisees and scribes turned their wrath toward Jesus. The dialogue that resulted provided some of the most revolutionary teachings of Christ. Three specific responses followed the observation of unwashed hands. The first confrontation was between Jesus and "the Pharisees and teachers of the law" (7:5–13). They asked a revealing question (7:5): "Why don't your disciples live according to the tradition of the elders . . . ?"

They asked a one-verse question, but Jesus gave them an eight-verse response.

As usual, Jesus spoke to the need of their hearts rather than to the question on their minds. He quoted the great prophet (Isaiah 29:13) in his response. He accused them of lip service, straying hearts, and vain worship (Mark 7:6–7). Along the way, he lowered the boom on them. "Hypocrites," he called them (7:6). Nothing could have been more biting. "Hypocrite" was a compound word meaning literally *to judge under*. The word became synonymous with *actor*, one who recites a script as if it was his or her own. These religious elite pretended to be holy and close to God, thus judging others as sinners.

Christ wasn't through. He moved from criticizing their motives to addressing their actions. "You have a fine way of setting aside the commands of God in order to observe your own traditions" (7:8). Jesus was not merely saying they had put their traditions on a level of *equality* with

> Evil intentions begin within.

God's word, but that they had put their traditions on a level *above* God's word. They considered that their traditions *surpassed* God's commands.

We, too, must choose between vain tradition and Scripture. We cannot follow both. It was one thing to "observe your own traditions," but far worse to set "aside the commands of God" (7:9). Unfortunately, many continue to embrace traditions over God's word.

Jesus next quoted Moses, a hero of the Pharisees and scribes, and addressed the vow of "Corban" (7:10–13). The practice of "Corban" was that of dedicating a gift for God's use. Many took a vow of "Corban" so as to dedicate money for religious purposes. The rabbis allowed the mere taking of the vow to prevent an unfaithful son from caring for his parents. Jesus said that the Pharisees and scribes had erred in two ways. First, they should have taken care of their parents with this money. Second, they often kept the money for personal use. The "Corban" vow put tradition ahead of God's word. Jesus accused the Pharisees and scribes of *nullifying* or voiding God's instructions (7:13).

Traditions can be helpful as long as they point to the truth and do not become a substitute for that truth.

Jesus' second response was directed to the crowd (7:14–15). He was clear. Being "unclean" was not an issue of unclean hands but of unclean hearts. Sin begins in the heart. This message on tradition versus internal activity was most revolutionary. Jeremiah said, "The heart is deceitful above all things and beyond cure" (Jeremiah 17:9). Jesus affirmed this dilemma six hundred years later. (Mark 7:16 does not appear in most recent translations since it does not appear in the earliest known manuscripts. It was likely added later in order to provide a natural conclusion to the text.)

Jesus provided a third message for the disciples (Mark 7:17–19). In private, they asked for further explanation of the parable in 7:14–15. Jesus must have been sad at the lack of depth among his closest followers. "'Are you so dull?' he asked" (7:18). Then he repeated his message (7:18): "Don't you see that nothing that enters a man from the outside can make him 'unclean'?"

Deadly Sins (7:20–23)

Jesus stated the focus of his message on this topic a third time: "What comes out of a man is what makes him 'unclean'" (7:20). Then Jesus offered a number of examples of sins that come from the heart. Evil intentions begin within.

Jesus began by mentioning "evil thoughts" and proceeded to name evil actions. "Sexual immorality" refers to illicit sexual activity, especially by the unmarried. The word "theft" describes taking something belonging to another. Jesus then reminded the disciples that both "murder" and "adultery" begin in the heart.

> . . . Jesus said that what defiles a person is a matter of the heart.

The remaining eight sins might seem less offensive, but all came from the same source, the heart (7:22). "Greed" is an urge for more, a crazed love of having things. "Malice" refers to the active pursuit of evil. "Deceit" means trickery or misleading actions. The word means to lure with bait or set a trap. By "lewdness,"

Jesus referred to unrestrained immorality that resents discipline.

The next sin of the heart is "envy," meaning covetousness. The word "envy" literally is *evil eye*, or focusing one's gaze on something that belongs to someone else. "Slander" means a desire to destroy a person's reputation. The Greek word is the word for *blasphemy.* "Arrogance" is a claim of superiority. The literal Greek word means *to show self above.* The final sin, "folly," means *to play the fool.* A foolish person failed to discern morality from immorality, the right way from the wrong way.

Jesus concluded his response with a restatement of his teaching. "All these evils come from inside and make a man unclean" (7:23).

Jesus had been asked one question, about handwashing. But he addressed the real question, about true cleansing. Jesus repeated the message five times (7:15, 19, 20, 21, 23). He wanted to be sure the Pharisees would have no doubt as to the place of oral tradition, God's true law, and the source of purity and sin. The Master engaged the Jewish elite in a revolutionary discussion they would not easily forget.

Implications and Actions

Traditions can be helpful as long as they point to the truth and do not become a substitute for that truth. Jesus rebuked the Pharisees for elevating oral tradition beyond God's commands. Five times Jesus said that what defiles a person is a matter of the heart. Our task is to give close attention to matters of the heart and to personal godliness.

Who Were These Guys?

Jesus experienced constant friction with the leaders of the Jews. Three of these are found in our text for this lesson—the Pharisees, the scribes, and the elders. Who were these guys?

- *The Pharisees.* This sect of the Jews was an authoritarian group of religious leaders. They advocated obedience to the oral law, or traditions. They believed Moses had given extra laws to the elders, who passed them on over a period of centuries. Since they sought to be esteemed for their personal piety, Jesus' accusation of hypocrisy was a stinging criticism.

- *The scribes.* Emerging four or five centuries before Christ, the scribes were a class of legal experts. They were not content with moral principles. They defined and amplified thousands of rules and regulations for every situation.

- *The elders.* The word "elder" meant *older*. This class of Jewish leaders can be seen beginning with the time of Moses (Exodus 3:16). They continued through much of the rest of the Old Testament era, especially in the time of the judges and the kings prior to the Exile. In the New Testament era, the elders were associated with the ruling body, the Sanhedrin.

Who Is a Hypocrite?

Jesus offered a biting criticism when he called the Pharisees "hypocrites" (Mark 7:6). A hypocrite is one who *acts the part.* The unchurched world is on the lookout for hypocrites within the church. How do we become hypocrites, or mere actors? Consider these, and you likely can think of others.

- We pay more attention to appearances than character.

- We carefully follow spiritual formulas, while our hearts are far from God.

- We choose to emphasize our virtues and others' sins.

Bringing It Home

- Can you identify any examples of hypocrisy in your life?

- What "Corban" vow have you made, but not kept? Renew your commitment to God today.

- Review the list of "deadly sins" in Mark 7:21–22. What are the areas in which you struggle most?

- Identify one thing you can do this week to keep your heart pure.

Questions

1. Why do you think the disciples, who were closest to Jesus, evidently did not understand these teachings any better than did the Pharisees or the crowd?

2. What traditions, good or bad, does your church cherish?

3. The Pharisees saw cleanliness (of hands) as next to godliness. In what similar legalistic ways do we measure godliness today?

4. What steps do you take to keep your heart clean?

5. In what ways could your class hold one another accountable to inner purity and righteousness?

Main Idea

We must open our eyes and
overcome our blind spots if
we are to see Jesus clearly
and respond accordingly.

Question to Explore

What would we be able to see
and understand about Jesus,
about ourselves, and about other
people if we would open our eyes
and overcome our blind spots?

There Are None So Blind

Study Aim

To analyze the blindness of
the Pharisees, the disciples,
and the blind man and to
identify implications for seeing
who Jesus is more clearly

Study and Action Emphases

- Affirm the Bible as our authoritative guide for life and ministry
- Share the gospel with all people
- Develop a growing, vibrant faith

Quick Read

The Pharisees, the disciples, and the helpless man all suffered from forms of blindness. Jesus used each situation to offer hope for anyone who seeks to see spiritual truth more clearly.

The revival service had just ended. Several adults had made first-time commitments to Christ. Our team of four stepped out of the church filled with praise and into the cold New England air. Once in the rental car, I promptly backed up through the parking lot.

My side mirror had a message for me. "Objects may be closer than they appear." That was a prophetic word! Sure enough, the area missionary's car was closer than it appeared. "I never saw it," I told my friend.

As a young driver, I once ran a stop sign. I told the nice officer, "I never saw it." Last year I entered an intersection as the traffic light mysteriously changed colors. "I never saw it," I told the sergeant. There have been other objects I "didn't see," such as speed limit signs, and "Wrong Way" and "Do Not Enter" signs. Through it all I have learned one valuable lesson. "I didn't see it" is a poor defense in traffic court.

I suffer from several ophthalmological (sight) maladies: near-sightedness, stigmatism, legal blindness in both eyes, and the worst ailment of all, being over forty years of age. My ophthalmologist loves me. I enjoy our time together. The drops that dilate my eyes are a blast. I love the giant search light he presses against my retina as he pleads, "Don't blink." I particularly enjoy the puff of air he shoots into my eye at 500 miles per hour. He says I need quadfocals (trifocals plus one). I refuse. So my doctor etched a permanent message on each eyeglass lens. "Objects may be closer than they appear."

Lesson 7: *There Are None So Blind*

Jesus fed 4,000 men a great lunch (Mark 8:1–10). By dinner time the crowd lost sight of who he was. The Pharisees wanted to see another sign. The disciples wanted to see who Jesus really was. The blind man just wanted to see. For all of them, the message was the same: *The Savior may be closer than he appears.*

Mark 8:11–26

¹¹The Pharisees came and began to question Jesus. To test him, they asked him for a sign from heaven. ¹²He sighed deeply and said, "Why does this generation ask for a miraculous sign? I tell you the truth, no sign will be given to it." ¹³Then he left them, got back into the boat and crossed to the other side.

¹⁴The disciples had forgotten to bring bread, except for one loaf they had with them in the boat. ¹⁵"Be careful," Jesus warned them. "Watch out for the yeast of the Pharisees and that of Herod."

¹⁶They discussed this with one another and said, "It is because we have no bread."

¹⁷Aware of their discussion, Jesus asked them: "Why are you talking about having no bread? Do you still not see or understand? Are your hearts hardened? ¹⁸Do you have eyes but fail to see, and ears but fail to hear? And don't you remember? ¹⁹When I broke the five loaves for the five thousand, how many basketfuls of pieces did you pick up?"

"Twelve," they replied.

20"And when I broke the seven loaves for the four thousand, how many basketfuls of pieces did you pick up?"

They answered, "Seven."

21He said to them, "Do you still not understand?"

22They came to Bethsaida, and some people brought a blind man and begged Jesus to touch him. **23**He took the blind man by the hand and led him outside the village. When he had spit on the man's eyes and put his hands on him, Jesus asked, "Do you see anything?"

24He looked up and said, "I see people; they look like trees walking around."

25Once more Jesus put his hands on the man's eyes. Then his eyes were opened, his sight was restored, and he saw everything clearly. **26**Jesus sent him home, saying, "Don't go into the village."

The Pharisees Who Couldn't See (8:11–13)

The religious leaders employed the timeless strategy of the enemy. They "began to question Jesus" (8:11). The attack usually starts with a question. The first temptation began with (Genesis 3:1), "Did God really say...?" Then, they asked for a sign, but their perspective was one of unbelief. They were not looking for validation of Christ's deity but for evidence to the contrary.

Their request seemed simple enough. "They asked him for a sign from heaven" (Mark 8:11). The request was out of place on several levels. First, they had already been given signs. Mark's Gospel records more than a dozen instances of public miracles prior to this plea for yet another sign. That is the problem with signs. When we are driven by signs, we always need more. God was already in the world, evident through his creation, faithfulness, prophets, and countless signs and miracles already performed.

Other problems with their request are apparent. The Pharisees were a walking contradiction. Just five chapters earlier, they had categorized Jesus' miracles as coming from Satan (3:22–30), but now they asked Jesus to perform a sign to prove his standing as Messiah. Another contradiction stands out. While asking Jesus to perform a sign that

The Pharisees could not see because of their legalistic and hypocritical ways.

would validate his divinity, they were demanding that he operate on their schedule. If Jesus was deity, he would not be subject to their demands. In that sense, if Jesus had performed a sign, his sovereignty might have been called into further question.

Jesus' response required only twenty-one words (8:12, NIV) and just a few seconds to hear! He did not enter into debate. There was no dialogue. He had better things to do than argue with the enemy. Similarly, Nehemiah ignored the attempts of Sanballat and Tobiah to hinder the building of the wall (Nehemiah 6:1–3). Paul focused on "one thing" (Philippians 3:13). Jesus knew his mission, and he stayed on track. He "sighed deeply" as before the healing of the deaf man (Mark 7:34). The sighs of Jesus in the Gospel of Mark came as he noted disease or moral failure. Imagine how Jesus must sigh over our culture today!

The Master said, "I tell you the truth . . ." (8:12), an assertion he repeated at other times in Mark's Gospel.[1] Then Jesus offered his brief reply. "No sign will be given to" this generation (8:12). He was not declaring a permanent moratorium on signs. Rather Jesus was saying there would be no more signs for "this generation." Christ knew that if he did give them another sign, they would still not believe. Worse still, they might "believe" for the wrong reason, seeking the sign of the Messiah rather than the Messiah of the sign. To a similar question in the Gospel of Matthew, Jesus said there would eventually be the "sign of the prophet Jonah" (Matthew 12:38–42), which would be the resurrection. Jesus spoke of the greater blessing reserved for those who believed without the benefit of a sign.

With that response, "he left them" (Mark 8:13). Few phrases are as sad as those three words. "He left them" serves as the epitaph for any people who choose not to bow before the one true God. The One who stands closer than he appears may move away without notice.

Unsightly Disciples (8:14–21)

While demons easily recognized Jesus for who he was, his disciples remained ignorant. Poor eyesight continued to plague them. They forgot to take enough bread for the journey (8:14).

Jesus used the bread as an object lesson. He warned his friends to "beware of the yeast of the Pharisees and that of Herod" (8:15). Yeast symbolized evil. The yeast, or leaven, was a piece of dough left over from a previous baking. The yeast caused the dough to rise, thus representing influence. Evil teachings ("yeast of the Pharisees") have the power to contaminate an entire society.

The Lord's warning specifically called out the Pharisees and Herod. The yeast of the Pharisees was hypocrisy (Luke 12:1). By "Herod," Jesus was referring to Herod Antipas, who sought his demise. Herod represented a spirit of secularism. The leaven

The disciples were blinded by the cares of daily life.

of Herod was bad politics, while the leaven of the Pharisees was bad theology. The connection of the Pharisees and Herod was their desire for an earthly kingdom.

Amazingly, after Jesus' teaching, the disciples reasoned, "It is because we have no bread" (Mark 8:16). They were blind to what Jesus was saying. Jesus confirmed that with his comment (8:17), "Do you still not see. . . ?"

The disciples' greater problem was not poor sight but hard hearts. The words of the prophets rang true for the generation of Jesus' day. "Hear this, you foolish and senseless people, who have eyes, but do not see, who have ears but do not hear" (Jeremiah 5:21). The people of Israel "have eyes to see but do not see and ears to hear but do not hear, for they are a rebellious people" (Ezekiel 12:2).

Jesus reminded the disciples of the two miracles of feeding the masses (Mark 8:19–20; see 6:30–44; 8:1–9). After the first feeding, twelve baskets of food remained. Seven baskets remained after the second miracle. As always, God more than meets our needs. Jesus

All of us are susceptible to spiritual blindness.

concluded with a final, penetrating question. "Do you still not understand?" (8:21). The disciples were focused on the lack of physical bread even though they were with the One who had just fed thousands of people on two occasions with a few loaves and fish.

The application of this passage is clear. The disciples—who ate, walked, and enjoyed life by Jesus' side—had no real vision of who he was. Even to those who should have seen Jesus for who he was, the Object was closer than he appeared.

Jesus' Most Unusual Healing (8:22–26)

The third portrayal of blindness focuses on Jesus' most unusual healing. It involved spit in the eye and required two "attempts" by the Healer before the man's sight was fully restored.

The text states, "They came to Bethsaida" (8:22). What followed was the second of two miracles unique to Mark (see 7:31–37 for the other).[2] A blind man was brought to Jesus. Blindness was a great curse of the East, often caused by various diseases, the glare of the sun, and poor hygiene.

Jesus "put saliva on his eyes" (8:23, NRSV), after leading him out of the town. Jesus touched the man and asked whether he could see "anything." Jesus knew the answer. Jesus did not ask whether the man could see *well* but whether he could see *anything.*

> *The man of Bethsaida suffered from physical blindness.*

The response seems odd, doesn't it? "I see people; they look like trees walking around" (8:24). The man's healing was not yet complete.

So Jesus put his hands on the man's eyes "once more" (8:25). Upon the second touch, "his eyes were opened, his sight was restored, and he saw everything clearly" (8:25). This two-phase miracle would stand as the only one of its kind in all of Jesus' ministry.

God's desire for his children is not merely that they have sight, but that they see clearly. Of course, Jesus could have provided complete healing and perfect vision instantaneously. For reasons unclear, he chose a two-step process.[3] Whatever the exact meaning, Mark saw fit to include this incident in the context of the disciples' failure to understand at first and their continued learning of who Jesus was.

As with Legion (5:19–20), Jesus then instructed the man to go home (8:26). Notice, Jesus "sent" him home. God's job is to tell us where to go, while our job is to obey. Jesus sent the man home rather than to an unfamiliar place where his testimony would be less dynamic. Jesus sent him home, rather than inviting him to join the Twelve. Jesus sent the man to share the good news of Jesus among those who knew the man best. Jesus told him, "Don't go into the village" (8:26). Jesus may have sought to delay the crisis that would be brought on by the uproar of a public miracle. Everything Jesus did, including sending this man home quietly, he did with his mission in mind. The man's silence was part of the plan by which Jesus revealed himself as the Christ who "must suffer" rather than as the nationalistic, militaristic Christ (8:31).

> The great opportunity of life is to see Jesus in all his glory.

> The good news is that Jesus is available.

Imagine the initial sight the formerly blind man experienced. Likely the first clear sight the man saw was Jesus. To a man who had lived his life in a world of darkness, Jesus was closer than he appeared.

Implications and Actions

Blindness comes in many forms. The Pharisees could not see because of their legalistic and hypocritical ways. The disciples were blinded by the cares of daily life. The man of Bethsaida suffered from physical blindness. For every form of blindness, Jesus was the cure.

All of us are susceptible to spiritual blindness. Healing may be immediate. But in these three stories, we see healing as a process. The great opportunity of life is to see Jesus in all his glory. The good news is that Jesus is available. He is closer than he often appears.

One Healing, Two Steps

The two-step healing of the blind man was unlike any other recorded miracle of Jesus. This story leaves several unanswered questions. Why did Jesus take him by the hand? Why did Jesus lead the man out of the village? What was the reason for using saliva? The most puzzling question is why Jesus healed in two steps. Consider these possibilities, and see whether you can think of others:

- Perhaps the man had incomplete faith.

- The two-step process served as an example of incremental spiritual growth.

- Jesus was slowly building the man's faith.

- Jesus wanted to provide two miraculous works, not just one.

- We need to understand that God works in many different ways.

Bringing It Home

- Think of something you see in Jesus now that you didn't see last year.

- List three things that tend to cloud your vision of Christ and his purpose for your life.

- Identify one "blind" person you can bring to Jesus this month.

- This week, write a card to a minister or friend who has helped you see Jesus more clearly this year.

Questions

1. Why was it so difficult for the Pharisees to see Jesus for who he really was?

2. After witnessing the feeding of the 4,000, why did the disciples lack understanding of who Jesus was?

3. Why do you think Jesus healed the blind man in two steps?

4. What steps can you take to see Jesus more clearly?

5. What implications does this study have about showing Jesus to a blind world?

NOTES

1. See Mark 3:28; 9:1, 41; 10:15, 29; 11:23; 12:43; 13:30; 14:9, 18, 25, 30.
2. Both miracles share interesting similarities. Jesus took both men away from the crowd, used saliva in the process, touched them, and told them to keep quiet about their healing.
3. Note that the next passage concerns Peter's confession of faith in Christ (8:27–29) and that the rest of the Gospel of Mark tells of events that continued to open the disciples' eyes.

THREE

With Jesus on the Way to the Cross

Unit three, "With Jesus on the Way to the Cross," follows Jesus and his disciples from Jesus' challenging question, "Who do you say I am?" (Mark 8:29), to the cross and the resurrection.[1] The emphasis of the passages selected for study is on the kind of discipleship to which Jesus calls his followers.

Lesson eight, "Not an Easy Way," is on Mark 8:27–38. It focuses on Jesus' explanation of the nature of discipleship.

Lesson nine, "Me First," is on Mark 9:30–37. In various ways in this passage, Jesus called his disciples to reject the approach of me first.

Lesson ten, "Disciple = Servant," is on Mark 10:32–45. There Jesus taught the crucial

129

importance of servanthood and pointed to the supreme example, himself.

Lesson eleven is a study of Mark 13. The emphasis of the study is on "Discipleship in Dangerous Times."

Lesson twelve, "Not Me," is from Mark 14:10–31, the account of Jesus' Last Supper with his disciples before the crucifixion. There Peter swore he would not deny Jesus, but he did. Do we?

Lesson thirteen, "The Worst and Best of Times," is on Jesus' crucifixion and resurrection, as described in Mark 14—16. The lesson will call us to consider how the event of the crucifixion and resurrection of Jesus affects our lives.

UNIT THREE. WITH JESUS ON THE WAY TO THE CROSS

Lesson 8	Not an Easy Way	Mark 8:27–38
Lesson 9	Me First	Mark 9:30–37
Lesson 10	Disciple = Servant	Mark 10:32–45
Lesson 11	Discipleship in Dangerous Times	Mark 13:1–13, 32–37
Lesson 12	Not Me	Mark 14:10–31
Lesson 13	The Worst and Best of Times	Mark 14:61b–64; 15:9–24, 37–41; 16:1–8

NOTES

1. Unless otherwise indicated, all Scripture quotations are from the New International Version.

Main Idea

The only proper place for a person to be is behind Jesus, following him, even though the way may not be easy.

Question to Explore

Where are you in relation to Jesus—ahead, behind, a long way away?

LESSON EIGHT

Not an Easy Way

Study Aim

To state the meaning of this passage for my life and to respond to Jesus by affirming or re-affirming my commitment to him

Study and Action Emphases

- Affirm the Bible as our authoritative guide for life and ministry
- Share the gospel with all people
- Develop a growing, vibrant faith
- Obey and serve Jesus by meeting physical, spiritual, and emotional needs
- Equip people for servant leadership

Quick Read

Following Jesus is not easy, but it is possible. Following Jesus, not getting ahead of him or lost from him, is possible when we know him, trust him, and admire him.

Several years ago I guided a group of people on a tour of the Holy Land. Many members of the group were older people who had not traveled extensively. I was thirty to forty years younger than most of them. But I had guided four tours of this land in previous years, and so I was not a novice. Before we visited the Old City of Jerusalem I instructed group members to follow me in order not to get lost. One tour member decided she wanted to go ahead of me to see some shops of interest. I reminded her twice not to go ahead of me for fear she would get lost. She evidently did not remember that I was to be trusted as the guide, and so she wandered ahead and was lost and alone until late in the evening when a sympathetic Arab taxi driver brought her to our hotel.

The Gospel of Mark presents us with an important truth concerning our relationship with Jesus. Through Jesus' encounter with Peter and other disciples we are confronted with our own understanding of who Jesus is as well as our willingness to follow him, even when following him is difficult.

Mark 8:27–38

27Jesus and his disciples went on to the villages around Caesarea Philippi. On the way he asked them, "Who do people say I am?"

28They replied, "Some say John the Baptist; others say Elijah; and still others, one of the prophets."

29"But what about you?" he asked. "Who do you say I am?"

Peter answered, "You are the Christ."

30Jesus warned them not to tell anyone about him.

31He then began to teach them that the Son of Man must suffer many things and be rejected by the elders, chief priests and teachers of the law, and that he must be killed and after three days rise again. **32**He spoke plainly about this, and Peter took him aside and began to rebuke him.

33But when Jesus turned and looked at his disciples, he rebuked Peter. "Get behind me, Satan!" he said. "You do not have in mind the things of God, but the things of men."

34Then he called the crowd to him along with his disciples and said: "If anyone would come after me, he must deny himself and take up his cross and follow me. **35**For whoever wants to save his life will lose it, but whoever loses his life for me and for the gospel will save it. **36**What good is it for a man to gain the whole world, yet forfeit his soul? **37**Or what can a man give in exchange for his soul? **38**If anyone is ashamed of me and my words in this adulterous and sinful generation, the Son of Man will be ashamed of him when he comes in his Father's glory with the holy angels."

Following Someone You Know (8:27–30)

Jesus asked his disciples this penetrating question (Mark 8:27): "Who do people say I am?" There was much speculation in first-century Israel about this man Jesus, about who he was and who he wasn't. The people in his hometown of Nazareth "took offense at him" (6:3). They discredited his teachings and accused him of being nothing more than a mere human being. The "teachers of the law" went so far as to say Jesus was doing the work of "the prince of demons" (3:22). His own disciples said that some thought Jesus was John the Baptist, Elijah, or one of the prophets (8:28). The question about who people said Jesus was was easy to answer.

But then came the second question (8:29): "Who do you say I am?" Only one word is different in the two questions, but that one word makes a crucial difference. This second question is no longer a question that can be answered with comfortable objectivity. This question cannot be satisfied with a simple intellectual response. This question has significant implications for our lives. How we answer this question Jesus asked will determine whether we will follow him. Will we follow someone we do not know?

Will we follow someone we do not know?

When Peter answered "You are the Christ" (8:29), he was affirming Old Testament prophecies about a promised Messiah, a chosen one. The English word *Christ* is a transliteration of the Greek word *christos*, defined as *anointed one*. The title "the Christ" was equivalent to the Hebrew word for *Messiah* (see John 1:41; 4:25). To be *anointed* was to be *chosen*. In the Old Testament, priests and kings were anointed with oil to show that they were chosen to lead God's people (see Exodus 30:30–31; 1 Samuel 9:16). In the New Testament, Jesus said that God had "anointed" him (Luke 4:18, quoting Isaiah 61:1–2). Peter preached that God had "anointed" Jesus with the Holy Spirit and with power (Acts 10:38). So when Peter answered in Mark 8:29 that Jesus was the Christ, he was acknowledging that he personally believed Jesus to be the Savior promised by God.

> *What is the connection between salvation and discipleship?*

Jesus immediately warned his disciples not to tell anyone that he was the Christ (8:30). He was always aware of and responsive to God's timing for his life and ministry (John 2:4; 17:1).

Following Someone You Trust (8:31–37)

After Jesus warned his disciples not to reveal his true identity, he began to tell them about his future. He told them that the Jewish religious leaders would turn against him and have him killed. But Jesus assured them that after three days he would rise from the dead (Mark 8:31; 9:31; 10:33–34).

Peter immediately rebuked Jesus about what Jesus said would happen (8:32). Matthew wrote that Peter said, "Never, Lord! . . . This shall never happen to you!" (Matthew 16:22). Even when Jesus later repeated his prediction, the disciples did not understand what Jesus meant by saying that he would be killed and after three days rise from the dead (Mark 9:32).

Jesus responded to Peter's rebuke by attributing that rebuke to Satan himself. He reminded Peter that Peter was thinking in worldly terms and not in heavenly or eternal terms (8:33). Jesus' vision came from God, and he was not going to have that vision clouded by Satan.

Jesus' rebuke to Peter was a reminder that Peter was to follow behind Jesus, not to get out in front of him or to wander away from him. Then Jesus taught his disciples what it meant to follow him. To follow Jesus meant self-denial, rejection, and self-sacrifice (8:34–35). Jesus' teaching on discipleship amplified the contrast Jesus made in his rebuke to Peter. To "have in mind . . . the things of men" meant to think like an unregenerate world thinks. It meant to try always to save one's life and to try to gain the whole world. It meant to avoid rejection, suffering, self-denial, and self-sacrifice. Jesus contrasted that mindset with having in mind "the things of God." Having in mind "the things of God" meant saying no to one's selfish desires even if doing so meant being rejected. Having in mind "the things of God" meant losing one's life

> *To be ashamed of Jesus means to be afraid to show an unbelieving world which side one is on.*

in service to God and the gospel. In losing one's life in service to God and the gospel, one would save his or her own "life" (referring to life in totality, temporal and eternal).

Neither Peter nor any other person could follow Jesus unless that person trusted Jesus. How could anyone believe that the meaning and purpose of life would be found in giving rather than in getting? How could anyone believe that genuine discipleship could be accomplished only through sacrificing long-established worldly beliefs? Either a person trusts what Jesus teaches and follows him or a person rejects what Jesus teaches and goes on ahead of him or wanders away from him.

Following Jesus' discourse on discipleship, the Gospel of Mark traces Jesus' journey to the cross. In this journey we see Jesus teaching and living out the realities of self-denial and rejection. He reminded the rich young ruler that the young man's possessions were standing between him and the kingdom (10:17–23). He told the disciples that anything they had given up in this age would be

Coming to an honest confession of Jesus as the Christ will help us to follow him rather than to walk ahead of him or walk away from him.

restored in plentiful fashion in the age to come (10:28–30). When the disciples James and John requested places of prominence in the kingdom, Jesus reminded them that what they were asking would require suffering and self-sacrifice (10:35–44). At the Passover meal, Jesus related to his followers the necessity of his personal sacrifice for them despite the betrayal of one of his own (14:17–25). Despite the fact that the disciples would sleep through Jesus' crucial time of prayer in the Garden of Gethsemane (14:32–42), and Peter would deny him (14:66–72), Jesus continued with perseverance to the cross. In all these ways Jesus taught and modeled what it meant to deny self and take up the cross.

Following Someone You Admire (8:38)

Jesus finished this discourse to his disciples with a strong statement about being "ashamed" of him and his words. Jesus knew that his teaching on discipleship would require more than many were willing to believe or give. Some would be ashamed to follow behind a leader who seemed weak to the point of giving in and giving up on the (seemingly) good things of life. Others would be ashamed to follow one who was being rejected by the majority, especially by the religious leaders of the day.

Trusting Jesus as the Christ will encourage us to follow his teachings of self-denial and self-sacrifice.

Jesus knew how important popularity and acceptance were to human beings. There would be those who would deny him during times of persecution. Yet Jesus made it plain that being ashamed of him now would cause him to be ashamed of them when he returned in glory. Their rejection of him in time would make it impossible for him to accept them in eternity. Their conduct toward him now would determine his conduct toward them when he returned. As William Barclay comments, "When the King comes into His Kingdom He will be loyal to those who have been loyal to Him. No man can expect to dodge all the trouble of some great undertaking and then to reap all the benefit of it."[1]

How significant is it to admire Jesus and his teachings? Jesus reminds us that the person who "acknowledges" him before other people he will "acknowledge" before God in heaven, but whoever "disowns" him before other people he will "disown" before God (Matt. 10:32–33).

What is the connection between salvation and discipleship? Sometimes the connection is referred to as *Lordship Salvation*. This expression means that one who does not do the work of the disciple cannot be a genuine follower of Jesus. It means that one who is ashamed of being a follower of

Admiring Jesus as the Christ will lead us to confess him openly before others.

Jesus to the point of ignoring the demands of discipleship, going ahead of Jesus instead of following him, cannot be saved (Matt. 7:21–23).

Mark 8:38 is complementary in structure to Mark 8:35. Thus, Mark 8:38 carries with it the judgment spoken of in 8:35, "will lose it" (life). When a person denies Christ because of basic anxiety about his or her life and an unwillingness to face the rejection of the world, that person denies Christ's ability to save.

Paul wrote that he was "not ashamed of the gospel, because it is the power of God for the salvation of everyone who believes . . ." (Romans 1:16). Paul used the same Greek word for "ashamed" that the Gospel of Mark uses in 8:38. Being "ashamed" of Jesus or his teachings would cause one to deny the very power of salvation. Jesus' words are words of life and the medium through which he communicates his plan for salvation. To be "ashamed" of Jesus' words means *to not believe them or accept them.*

Being ashamed of Jesus means to do the opposite of what Jesus taught (see 8:34). It means to deny Jesus, to prefer the values of the world, and to turn from him. To be ashamed of Jesus means to walk ahead of or away from Jesus. To be ashamed of Jesus means to be afraid to show an unbelieving world which side one is on.

Implications and Actions

Coming to an honest confession of Jesus as the Christ will help us to follow him rather than to walk ahead of him or walk away from him. Trusting Jesus as the Christ will encourage us to follow his teachings of self-denial and self-sacrifice. Admiring Jesus as the Christ will lead us to confess him openly before others.

Faithful in Spite of Challenges

Z.N. Morrell crossed the Sabine River into Texas in 1835 to be a pioneer preacher of the gospel. He was later called the greatest pioneer preacher in Texas and one of the greatest in America. As he struck out to establish the gospel in Texas, he took Isaiah 35:1 and applied that verse to Texas: "The desert shall rejoice, and blossom as the rose" (KJV).

When Morrell would become discouraged, he would say, "My heart is fixed. God gave me an inward token . . . that he would recognize my offerings in years to come. The wilderness would yet blossom as the rose." Even though Morrell faced many challenges, he laid "solid Baptist foundations" and did not waver in his vision.[2]

Applying Jesus' Teachings

To apply these teachings of Jesus to your life:
- List those areas where you are tempted to save your own life.
- Meditate on things you might try to exchange for your life.
- Identify some occasions for you to take up your cross and follow Jesus.
- Look for times when you can openly confess your faith in Jesus.

Questions

1. Why do you think Jesus warned his disciples not to tell anyone he was the Christ?

2. What caused Peter to rebuke Jesus about Jesus' prediction of what would happen to him?

3. How do you share with people who you think Jesus is?

4. What are some barriers you face in following Jesus?

5. What teaching of Jesus would cause one to be tempted to be ashamed of him?

NOTES

1. William Barclay, *The Gospel of Mark*, The Daily Study Bible (Philadelphia: The Westminster Press, 1956), 213.
2. Harry Leon McBeth, *Texas Baptists: A Sesquicentennial History* (Dallas, Texas: BAPTISTWAY PRESS, 1998), 15–18.

Main Idea

The attitude of *me first* must be changed radically if we are to be faithful in following Jesus.

Question to Explore

So what's the problem with *me first*? Isn't that the way the world works?

LESSON NINE

Me First

Study Aim

To identify ways in which Jesus called for a radical change in the idea of *me first*

Study and Action Emphases

- Affirm the Bible as our authoritative guide for life and ministry
- Develop a growing, vibrant faith
- Include all God's family in decision-making and service
- Value all people as created in the image of God
- Encourage healthy families
- Equip people for servant leadership

Quick Read

Jesus took his disciples' desire for greatness and redirected it from *me first* to *others first*. He used a child to illustrate the nature of Christian service, teaching that serving the least and most helpless in society is in reality serving God.

One of our favorite games in elementary school was *King of the Mountain*. A group of second-grade boys would struggle with one another to see who could stay on top of a small dirt pile we considered *the mountain*. The purpose of the game was to be the lone person standing on the top of the mountain. In order to be the lone person standing on the top of the mountain, one had to conquer all the others trying to get there. The nature of the game was winning or out-competing all challengers for the top. It boiled down to *me first*!

Mark 9:30–37

30They left that place and passed through Galilee. Jesus did not want anyone to know where they were, 31because he was teaching his disciples. He said to them, "The Son of Man is going to be betrayed into the hands of men. They will kill him, and after three days he will rise." 32But they did not understand what he meant and were afraid to ask him about it.

33They came to Capernaum. When he was in the house, he asked them, "What were you arguing about on the road?" 34But they kept quiet because on the way they had argued about who was the greatest.

35Sitting down, Jesus called the Twelve and said, "If anyone wants to be first, he must be the very last, and the servant of all."

36He took a little child and had him stand among them. Taking him in his arms, he said to them,

37 "Whoever welcomes one of these little children in my name welcomes me; and whoever welcomes me does not welcome me but the one who sent me."

In the Background (9:1–29)

The disciples had tasted a sense of Jesus' power by witnessing the phenomenal event of his transfiguration (Mark 9:2–13). The experience was so wonderful that Peter suggested building shelters and staying on the mountain. Instead, Jesus departed with them to go back down the mountain. On the way down the mountain, Jesus talked about "rising from the dead," a subject that puzzled his disciples (9:10). Another subject that puzzled the disciples was the question of the coming of Elijah, the same Elijah who had appeared with Jesus in the transfiguration. According to Malachi 4:5–6, Elijah would come just before the great day of the Lord. Jesus told his disciples that Elijah had come already in the person of John the Baptizer (Mark 9:13; see Matthew 11:13–14).

. . . Those people who kept their strength and sanity the longest were those who tried to help other prisoners and share what little they had.

Following this teaching about Elijah, the disciples became involved in an argument with the teachers of the law over the disciples' inability to heal a boy. After asking his disciples what they were arguing about with the teachers of the law, Jesus healed the boy. When the disciples asked why they had been unable to heal him, Jesus explained that the evil spirit that brought about the boy's problem could "come out only by prayer" (Mark 9:29).

Discipleship Training on the Way to the Cross (9:30–32)

As Jesus and his disciples "passed through Galilee … he was teaching his disciples" (9:30–31). What he was teaching was the hard lesson he had begun to teach them in 8:31 and for which Peter had rebuked Jesus. The disciples still "did not understand," as the next incident would show (9:32).

The Greatness Complex (9:33–34)

Muhammad Ali was one of the greatest boxers who ever climbed into the ring. He was well-known for his personal description of himself: "I am the greatest!" He was both admired and vilified because of that statement, and yet his personal ability as a boxer seemed to prove it. As one sportscaster said, "It ain't bragging if you can do it."

Jesus did not scold his disciples for wanting to be great. He wants all his followers to be great. His reply to the disciples was simple, "If anyone wants to be first . . ." (9:35). He was implying that wanting to have a life noted for significance or wanting to have a life of achievement is not necessarily wrong. In fact, in Jesus' parable of the talents (Matt. 25:14–30), Jesus commended the servants who worked hard and doubled what had been entrusted to them. He condemned the servant who played it safe and hid his money in the ground. Jesus' response to their argument over greatness must have surprised the disciples.

Ministry energizes us, contrary to the fear that our resources will be depleted in helping others.

Earlier, when Jesus had asked his disciples what they were arguing about on the road, they kept quiet. They were probably embarrassed about being caught in the grips of self-seeking glory. To hear Jesus affirm their desire for greatness might have relieved their embarrassment. By entering into this discussion with his disciples, Jesus showed his disciples that he was interested in their struggle and wanted to help them satisfy the desire for greatness in the right way.

Rather than attacking his disciples for having aspirations for greatness, Jesus began to teach them how to satisfy those aspirations in the proper way. He taught them that the idea of *me first* had to be radically changed. This would require them to put into action what Jesus had taught in Mark 8:34–37—to deny themselves. This lesson would be another part of discipleship training on the way to the cross.

The Necessity of Humility (9:35)

Jesus' instructions on satisfying the human desire for greatness would be the opposite of those popularly accepted in the first century—or in any century. Greatness among the world rulers of the day was achieved by the domination of others. The great ones were the ones who "lord it over" others (Matt. 20:25). Greatness was found on the top of the moun-

> *. . . Spiritual greatness is found, not in winning, but in making others winners—in putting others first.*

tain, and the way to get there was to out-compete everyone else, to climb over everyone else's back at their expense.

Jesus rejected this kind of greatness. He told his disciples that true greatness in the kingdom of God began with a willingness to be last, not first. He said to them, "If anyone wants to be first, he must be the very last . . ." (Mark 9:35). Jesus was teaching that a disciple must will himself to be the very last. One makes such a choice by faith in Jesus Christ. One of the disciples who heard this teaching, Peter, later wrote, "God opposes the proud but gives grace to the humble" (1 Peter 5:5, quoting Proverbs 3:34). He also wrote, "Humble yourselves, therefore, under God's mighty hand, that he may lift you up in due time" (1 Pet. 5:6). The willingness to step to the end of the line is a spiritual discipline and a mark of a true disciple.

Dr. Viktor Frankl was an Austrian physician who was imprisoned in one of Adolf Hitler's death camps. He and his fellow Jewish people suffered unbelievable atrocities. Everything about their living and working conditions was deplorable, including medical care. Dr. Frankl offered medical help, meager though it was in that terrible situation, to the sick and dying. Over time he discovered a unique phenomenon. He noticed that those people who kept their strength and sanity the longest were those who tried to help other prisoners and share what little they had. Their physical and mental condition seemed strengthened by their friendliness, compassion, and focus on something other than themselves.[1]

> *Genuinely being a servant is the opposite of* me first.

What Dr. Frankl discovered in his observations in the death camp was what Jesus was teaching his disciples. Ministry energizes us, contrary to the fear that our resources will be depleted in helping others. Genuinely being a servant is the opposite of *me first*.

Being a disciple of Jesus does not exempt one from the craving for notoriety, position, recognition, or power. Those closest to Jesus—the ones who touched him and heard him teach—struggled with this desire to have power over others, to be recognized as first in the kingdom. Jesus taught them, though, that spiritual greatness is found, not in winning, but in making others winners—in putting others first.

The earthly kingdom finds where people are vulnerable and hurts them. The kingdom of God finds where people are vulnerable and helps them.

A young man working in a human needs ministry in Orlando, Florida, told about a day in his ministry when he saw the face of Jesus. The line of people waiting to get food was long that day. At the very end of the line was a young girl who appeared to be about twelve years of age.

. . . He would always believe he saw the face of God that day.

She waited patiently as those at the front of the line received some rice, canned goods, and a couple of pieces of fruit. Slowly but surely, she made her way to the front of the line and closer to the food. From time to time she would glance across the street. The people serving the food noticed with concern that they were running out of food. The young girl kept looking across the street at three little figures huddled together under a tree. As she stepped forward to get her food, the only thing left was a banana. The workers were embarrassed to tell her that the banana was all they had. But she didn't mind and seemed happy to get the banana. The workers watched as she ran across the street where the three small children were waiting. Very deliberately she peeled the banana and divided it into three equal parts. She handed one piece of banana to each child. For her own meal, she licked the inside of the banana peel. This worker said he would always believe he saw the face of God that day.

Serving *All* (9:35–37)

Jesus taught that in putting others first, one had to become "the servant of all" (Mark 9:35). Becoming a servant of *all* is not an easy task. Becoming a servant of *some* may be rewarding. Becoming a servant of *some* may be fun and fulfilling. But being a servant of *all* is another question.

Jesus used the illustration of a little child to emphasize that the *all* included those who were basically helpless and could do nothing in return. Where is the payoff in helping these kinds of people? Jesus taught that every deed done in his name would be rewarded (9:41). On these

The path to greatness . . . puts others first rather than putting me first.

occasions we have to place our faith in God that God will see and reward what is done. Paul taught that we should always give ourselves "fully" to the work of Jesus because our "labor in the Lord" would never be "in vain" (1 Corinthians 15:58). Paul also wrote, "Serve wholeheartedly, as if you were serving the Lord, not men, because you know that the Lord will reward everyone for whatever good he does, whether he is slave or free" (Ephesians 6:7–8).

The second chapter of Philippians tells of the perfect example of a servant. Jesus "made himself nothing" (Philippians 2:7). This is called the *kenotic* passage, from the Greek word *kenosis*, meaning *to empty*. Jesus emptied himself of any right to be first and took "the very nature of a servant." This humility first led Jesus to the cross, but it ultimately led him to resurrection and exaltation. He willingly made himself last, and God rewarded him by making him first!

Becoming a "servant of all" means we have to empty ourselves of any pretense of being better than any other person. We have to be willing to serve all people regardless of status, race, gender, or religion. Serving the least among us is like serving Jesus himself. God will take the service and turn it into blessing.

While I was a seminary student, I saw a beautiful illustration of the rewards of serving the least. A fellow student called me one day to ask whether I had any debt I could not pay. I told him that I owed more than $200 on a gasoline bill and I was able to pay only the minimum each month. He told me to give him the bill and consider it paid. I was shocked. I asked how he could do this since he was a struggling seminary student as well. He told how he and his wife had allowed a couple to live with them, rent free, while that couple searched for a job. The husband in the couple found a job and over the years had become very successful and wealthy. He had remembered the kindness of this student and sent him a check for more than $5,000. The student had done his act of kindness many years before without any thought of reward. But God remembered!

The path to greatness leads to serving Christ through serving the least.

Implications and Actions

Jesus does not condemn our desire to be great. Instead, he teaches how his disciples are to satisfy that desire through humility and service. The path to greatness runs through humility and service and puts *others first* rather than putting *me first*. The path to greatness leads to serving Christ through serving the least.

Applying Jesus' Teachings

- Make a list of ways to put others—including people in your family—first in daily activities.

- Volunteer to work in a food kitchen or other ministry to the poor.

- Keep a journal of the times you push yourself forward to try to get first place.

- Reward someone who has done something nice for you.

Questions

1. What are some of your ambitions for greatness?

2. What are some examples of God frustrating your drive for greatness?

3. What is one instance in which you deliberately chose the back of the line over the front?

4. What is a good way to serve the least in your community?

5. In the phrase "servant of all" (9:35), who are some of the "all" who often are rejected by religious people?

6. What is an example of God rewarding your humble service?

NOTES

1. Viktor E. Frankl, *Man's Search for Meaning*, rev. ed. (New York: Washington Square Press, 1984).

Main Idea

To be a genuine disciple of Jesus is to be a servant, not a master, of all.

Question to Explore

Are you a servant? How did you feel the last time someone treated you like one?

LESSON TEN

Disciple = Servant

Study Aim

To decide how I will respond to Jesus' teachings on servanthood

Study and Action Emphases

- Affirm the Bible as our authoritative guide for life and ministry
- Share the gospel with all people
- Develop a growing, vibrant faith
- Obey and serve Jesus by meeting physical, spiritual, and emotional needs
- Equip people for servant leadership

Quick Read

While Jesus was on his way to the cross, two of his disciples came to him seeking places of prominence in the kingdom. Jesus reminded them that his disciples were to be servants, not masters. He himself would set the example of service, even to the point of giving his life.

Would they ever "get it"? Will we?

For the third time, Jesus shared with his disciples that he would be persecuted and killed but that he would rise from the dead three days later (Mark 10:32–34; see 8:31; 9:31). The disciples heard what Jesus said but did not grasp its significance.

Even after hearing all these things, two of the disciples, James and John, requested that they be given seats of honor next to Jesus when he came into his kingdom. They were continuing to focus on an earthly kingdom that they believed Jesus' might and power would bring into being.

Mark 10:32–45

32They were on their way up to Jerusalem, with Jesus leading the way, and the disciples were astonished, while those who followed were afraid. Again he took the Twelve aside and told them what was going to happen to him. **33**"We are going up to Jerusalem," he said, "and the Son of Man will be betrayed to the chief priests and teachers of the law. They will condemn him to death and will hand him over to the Gentiles, **34**who will mock him and spit on him, flog him and kill him. Three days later he will rise."

35Then James and John, the sons of Zebedee, came to him. "Teacher," they said, "we want you to do for us whatever we ask."

36"What do you want me to do for you?" he asked.

Lesson 10: Disciple = Servant

37They replied, "Let one of us sit at your right and the other at your left in your glory."

38"You don't know what you are asking," Jesus said. "Can you drink the cup I drink or be baptized with the baptism I am baptized with?"

39"We can," they answered.

Jesus said to them, "You will drink the cup I drink and be baptized with the baptism I am baptized with, **40**but to sit at my right or left is not for me to grant. These places belong to those for whom they have been prepared."

41When the ten heard about this, they became indignant with James and John. **42**Jesus called them together and said, "You know that those who are regarded as rulers of the Gentiles lord it over them, and their high officials exercise authority over them. **43**Not so with you. Instead, whoever wants to become great among you must be your servant, **44**and whoever wants to be first must be slave of all. **45**For even the Son of Man did not come to be served, but to serve, and to give his life as a ransom for many."

In the Background (10:1–31)

The Pharisees had tried to test Jesus by asking him whether it was "lawful for a man to divorce his wife" (10:1–12). Jesus restated God's creative purpose for marriage and later strengthened it with the teaching on adultery when he addressed his disciples' questions.

In verses 13–16, Jesus' disciples rebuked people for bringing little children to him. Maybe the disciples thought Jesus was too busy to be taking time with children. Maybe they considered him too big a personality to be taking time with them. Maybe they thought the little children were not important to Jesus. They were wrong.

Then, when Jesus told a man of "great wealth" to sell everything he had so that he could inherit eternal life, the man "went away sad" (10:22). Jesus was emphasizing how easy it is for wealth to get in the way of eternal values. He reminded his disciples that anyone who had given up things or relationships to follow him would ultimately be rewarded many times over. Jesus wanted them to understand that they were giving something they could not keep to get something they could not lose.

> *Living the lifestyle of a servant of Jesus Christ means living a life in constant awareness of the desires of God and the needs of people.*

Blinded By Personal Ambition (10:32–38a)

While Jesus was preparing to die for the disciples, they were struggling over positions of power and recognition. He was concerned with giving his life to save humankind, and they were concerned with saving a place of importance for themselves. Nothing hinders the work of God more than the petty fighting over position and recognition by those who claim to know Jesus as Savior and Lord. In the parable of the wedding feast (Luke 14:7–11), Jesus warned his followers that wanting to be first or prominent would lead to humiliation.

James and John were looking to the day when Jesus would be victorious and would set up his kingdom. They were thinking in terms of an earthly kingdom. They wanted to be given the prime seats next to Jesus. Maybe they thought they were entitled to these seats.

Service is at the heart of the Christian faith.

After all, Jesus had brought them into the inner circle several times (Mark 5:37; 9:2). The special attention they had been given by the Master himself may have led them to have a higher estimation of their place in the kingdom.

I am reminded of a pastor who had preached an effective sermon one Sunday morning and was showered with accolades. While driving home from church with his wife, he asked her, "Honey, how many really great preachers do you think there are in our denomination?" His wife replied, "One less than you think." Ouch! She was right on target, though.

Personal ambition becomes a barrier to greatness in the kingdom of God. This attitude can be seen in 3 John 9. The passage points out a troublemaker in the church. His name was Diotrephes, and he is described as one "who loves to be first." Diotrephes's desire to be first drove him to gossip maliciously about others and to refuse to "welcome" others into the church.

Personal ambition can blind one to following Jesus Christ. Being a disciple of Jesus Christ necessitates that one be willing to serve everyone rather than wanting to be master of everyone.

Maybe they thought the little children were not important to Jesus. They were wrong.

The appeal to personal ambition is one of the strong temptations of the devil. As Jesus began his ministry, the devil came to him in the wilderness to offer him power, prestige, and ease (Luke 4:1–13). The only thing Jesus had to do to get these things was to compromise God's plan for his life. That compromise would have cost Jesus his ultimate purpose in life. He rebuked the devil at every point by citing Scripture that redirected himself to the will of God.

In 2 Corinthians 12:1–10, the Apostle Paul related how God dealt with Paul's tendency to become conceited over the tremendous personal revelations God had given him. In order to help Paul become a more effective servant of the gospel, God gave him "a thorn in [his] flesh" to keep him humble. The "thorn" kept Paul's personal ambition in check by causing him to rely on the power of God's grace rather than his own native abilities.

The rewards for serving others far outweigh the recognition for having others serve us. God sees every act of service we offer and makes certain none of it is wasted (1 Corinthians 15:58). His reward for service is eternal while earthly recognition and fame is fleeting (1 Cor. 3:10–15).

Bearing the Burdens of Jesus (10:38b–40)

The Scriptures make it clear that Christians are not only going to reign with Jesus but also to suffer for him (Philippians 1:29). The disciples, like the Jewish leaders of Jesus' day, believed that the Messiah would bring power, glory, and conquest. The connection of a Messiah and suffering was incredible to them.

Jesus wanted them to understand that they were giving something they could not keep to get something they could not lose.

The same is true in our day. Some preachers and teachers teach a theology of avoidance. This theology teaches that God wants to give his children everything so that they can avoid deprivation and suffering in every area of life. What this theology misses is at the heart of the Christian faith—discipline, sacrifice, and suffering.

One of life's greatest temptations is to avoid doing the hard things. In Jesus' wilderness experience prior to his public ministry, the devil came to him to offer him an opportunity to avoid the hard things in life and ministry—discipline, sacrifice, and suffering (Matthew 4:1–11). But Jesus refused to take the easy route, recognizing that to do so would cause him to miss out on God's ultimate plan for his life.

A myth prevalent in our society says life is better if it is easier. But experience teaches us that there is no growth—physically, mentally, or emotionally—without struggle. It may well be that three of the worst liabilities a person can possess are natural physical attractiveness, natural ability, and inherited wealth. Each one brings with it a sense of entitlement. With such qualities, little or no effort may be required to get to where one wants to go. But the downside is that many people with these gifts spend all of life going nowhere.

> *The rewards for serving others far outweigh the recognition for having others serve us.*

Similar to this myth in our society, a spiritual myth teaches that spiritual life is better if it is easier. Some Christians seem to want to do as little as possible but expect to get as much as possible. However, there is no spiritual growth without struggle (Romans 5:3–5). Christian character is built in our struggles. In our struggles, we meet the God who is able to deliver us and make us stronger (Rom. 8:28).

Jesus made it clear that the disciples would indeed suffer with him. They would "drink the cup" he would drink (Mark 10:38). This "cup" is the one Jesus referred to as he prayed in the Garden of Gethsemane (14:36). The cup was Jesus' suffering and death. Too, the "baptism" (10:38) was his death, burial, and all that went with it. The disciples would indeed suffer because of the suffering and death of Jesus. Jesus, though, would not usurp God's sovereignty over what position his disciples would occupy in the kingdom (10:40). His purpose for coming to earth was to do the will of God, and the will of God was the final word (John 6:39).

In Mark 8:34–37, Jesus had taught his disciples that anyone who wanted to follow him or be his disciple must commit to a life of self-denial and cross-bearing. The self-denial Jesus was talking about could be denying one's dependence on saving oneself. It could also be the denial of self-ish ambitions. The rich young man who came to Jesus seeking eternal life was unwilling to deny himself the security of his

Personal ambition can blind one to following Jesus Christ.

money. However, self-denial and asceticism are not synonymous. An ascetic is one who denies himself any pleasure. Jesus was not an ascetic (Matt. 11:19). The self-denial Jesus is describing is anything that puts self before Jesus in any of life's ambitions.

To take up one's cross means to be willing to give one's life totally for Jesus Christ. It means more than undergoing hardship. It means self-sacrifice for the cause of Christ. Simon Peter tried to keep Jesus from going to the cross (Mark 8:32), but Jesus rebuked him by saying, "You do not have in mind the things of God, but the things of men" (8:33). Had Peter been successful in keeping Jesus from the cross, he would have caused Jesus to miss his life's purpose. Jesus

169

would have lost his life by saving it. Having in mind "the things of men" means always watching out for one's self-interests. It means trying to always come out on top. Bearing one's cross means giving up one's selfish ambitions to the ambitions of Jesus Christ.

Real life is found in giving one's life for the sake of the gospel. It is perfectly possible for people to gain all the things they have set their hearts on and then awaken one morning to find that they have missed the most important things of all. Then there is no amount of money that can buy back the lost years and lost opportunities. The standard of greatness in the kingdom is the standard of the cross.

> *Real life is found in giving one's life for the sake of the gospel.*

Becoming Great in the Kingdom (10:41–45)

Jesus pointed out that the cultural model of leadership and greatness was one of dominance and authority. The Gentiles wanted to be masters rather than servants. But Jesus quickly refuted that model for his disciples. He taught them that greatness in the kingdom came through service to all. He reinforced this teaching by noting that he came to serve and give his life for others rather than to be served (10:45).

In John 13:15, Jesus said to his disciples that he was leaving them an example to follow. The example Jesus left for his disciples to follow was washing each other's feet, which was the work of a servant. When Peter protested that Jesus would not wash his feet, Jesus responded by telling Peter that if Peter didn't let him wash his feet Peter would have "no part with" him. Peter could see no value in sacrifice. From Peter's perspective, giving one's life was a loss. From Jesus' perspective, giving his life was the only way to gain humankind's salvation.

Implications and Actions

Taking the position of a servant means sacrificing one's place as a master. It means removing self as the ruling principle of life. It means making Jesus Christ and his work the ruling principle of life. Becoming a servant may mean sacrificing prestige in order to serve God in an out-of-the-way place or to do the small thing. Jesus told his disciples

The standard of greatness in the kingdom is the standard of the cross.

that "whoever welcomes a little child like this in my name welcomes me" (Matt.18:5). Living the lifestyle of a servant of Jesus Christ means living a life in constant awareness of the desires of God and the needs of people. Service is at the heart of the Christian faith.

The final judgment of the nations is described in Matthew 25:31–46. In this parable Jesus described what would separate the sheep and the goats in the kingdom of God. We don't find some complicated theological formula for determining the sheep and the goats. What we find is simple acts of kindness done to the most needy in our world. Service to those who can't serve us in return is what Jesus demands.

Servant

The Greek New Testament uses two words that can be translated *servant*. The words are *diakonos* and *doulos*. Jesus used both words in what he taught the disciples in Mark 10:43–44, "Not so with you. Instead, whoever wants to become great among you must be your servant, and whoever wants to be first must be your slave. . . ." The slave (Greek, *doulos*) is lower than the servant (Greek, *diakonos*). A *diakonos* is one who intentionally serves another. The *doulos* is a slave who takes orders from a master. The word *diakonos*, meaning *servant* or *minister*, is used in Mark 9:35.

As a Ransom

Jesus said that he came "to give his life as a ransom for many" (Mark 10:45). The Greek word for ransom is *lutron*, referring to the price paid for release of someone held in bondage. The ransom of Jesus was paid for our sin and guilt. This act released us from its bondage (see John 1:29). Our sin and guilt held us liable to the penalty due from God, eternal death (Romans 6:23).

Jesus paid the ransom to God, against whom we have sinned, in the only way it could be paid, with his life given in death (Matthew 26:28; Ephesians 1:7). God alone has the power to inflict the penalty on us. The ransom was paid for the "many" by the death of one, the Son of Man. Jesus paid the price for all people (1 Timothy 2:5–6). His death brought about our redemption. His death set aside the need for animal or other sacrifices and established "once for all" the sacrifice that would provide salvation for those who believe (Hebrews 10:5–10). The "ransom" Jesus paid provided the new covenant or agreement between God and his people—a covenant of forgiveness based on God's grace (Matt. 26:28).

Naming Rights?

A church is making plans to build a new sanctuary. The long-range planning committee has done their work and presents the plan to the congregation. The plan is unanimously accepted. During the fund-raising phase, a member suggests selling naming rights for certain parts of the building, giving special recognition to those who give substantial sums of money. How would you respond to that suggestion, knowing that many people will be giving as much as they can without any thought of public recognition?

Questions

1. How can we be servants without being doormats?

2. How can we apply Jesus' teaching on servanthood in the local church?

3. How can we apply Jesus' teaching in the world
    of work where we may be in a management or
    supervisory position?

Main Idea

When disciples face opposition and even the threat of death, they are to continue to be faithful witnesses for Jesus, relying on the Spirit's power.

Question to Explore

How far should we really be willing to go for this Christianity thing?

LESSON ELEVEN

Discipleship in Dangerous Times

Study Aim

To evaluate the seriousness of my commitment to Jesus and to commit myself to being faithful

Study and Action Emphases

- Affirm the Bible as our authoritative guide for life and ministry
- Share the gospel with all people
- Develop a growing, vibrant faith

Quick Read

Being faithful means staying with a task or a commitment until it is completed. The commitment to being a disciple of Jesus Christ calls for faithfulness to Jesus and his task in the face of opposition, suffering, and even death.

While serving as an associate pastor of an inner-city church some years ago, I was involved in an extensive bus ministry. We provided transportation for people who had no other way to come to church. One person who rode the bus was a young boy about ten years of age. He was so thrilled to get to ride the bus to Sunday School and church. Doing so provided a chance to get out of a desperately poor neighborhood and receive some special attention from his teachers.

One Sunday this young boy professed his faith in Jesus Christ. The next week I visited him in his home, which was a garage apartment with a dirt floor. His mother was very angry with his decision and refused to let him be baptized. I found out later that this young boy's mother gave him a beating after I left the apartment. That someone would actually suffer in America for professing faith in Jesus Christ was hard for me to believe. But it is exactly what Jesus promised for some who would follow him.

Jesus continued to teach and to work miracles among the people as he traveled with his disciples to Jerusalem for his date with crucifixion and resurrection. During this time (Mark 10:46—12:44), he

- healed blind Bartimaeus
- rode into Jerusalem on a colt to the adulation of the crowd
- cursed a fig tree for not being fruitful
- drove out those who were selling merchandise in the temple courts

- taught about the power of faith and the necessity of forgiveness
- dealt with the proper commitments to church and state
- cleared up questions about marriage at the resurrection
- emphasized the greatest commandment
- delighted the crowd by referring to the teaching of David concerning the Christ
- warned about the pomposity of the teachers of the law
- commended a poor widow for her generous offering

Mark 13:1–13, 32–37

1As he was leaving the temple, one of his disciples said to him, "Look, Teacher! What massive stones! What magnificent buildings!"

2"Do you see all these great buildings?" replied Jesus. "Not one stone here will be left on another; every one will be thrown down."

3As Jesus was sitting on the Mount of Olives opposite the temple, Peter, James, John and Andrew asked him privately, **4**"Tell us, when will these things happen? And what will be the sign that they are all about to be fulfilled?"

5Jesus said to them: "Watch out that no one deceives you. **6**Many will come in my name, claiming, 'I am he,' and will deceive many. **7**When you hear of wars and rumors of wars, do not be alarmed. Such things must happen, but the end is still to come. **8**Nation will rise against nation, and kingdom against kingdom. There will be earthquakes in various places, and famines. These are the beginning of birth pains.

9"You must be on your guard. You will be handed over to the local councils and flogged in the synagogues. On account of me you will stand before governors and kings as witnesses to them. **10**And the gospel must first be preached to all nations. **11**Whenever you are arrested and brought to trial, do not worry beforehand about what to say. Just say whatever is given you at the time, for it is not you speaking, but the Holy Spirit.

12"Brother will betray brother to death, and a father his child. Children will rebel against their parents and have them put to death. **13**All men will hate you because of me, but he who stands firm to the end will be saved.

• • • • • • • • • • • • • • • • • • • •

32"No one knows about that day or hour, not even the angels in heaven, nor the Son, but only the Father. **33**Be on guard! Be alert! You do not know when that time will come. **34**It's like a man going away: He leaves his house and puts his servants in charge, each with his assigned task, and tells the one at the door to keep watch.

35"Therefore keep watch because you do not know when the owner of the house will come back—whether in the evening, or at midnight, or when the rooster crows, or at dawn. **36**If he comes suddenly, do not let him find you sleeping. **37**What I say to you, I say to everyone: 'Watch!'"

Questions

Mark 13 contains Jesus' response to the admiration of one of his disciples for the magnificence of the temple. As Jesus talked about the coming destruction of the temple, Peter, James, John, and Andrew asked Jesus two questions (Mark 13:4): "When will these things happen? . . . What will be the sign that they are all about to be fulfilled?"

The first question relates to the destruction of the temple and the second to the end of the age. Jesus answered these questions by saying that only God knows when the events described in Mark 13 will occur but that there would be signs that pointed toward the occurrences. The only certain sign Jesus gave for the end was that the gospel would have to be preached to "all nations" (13:10). The word translated "nations" is translated from the Greek word *ethne*, which can also be rendered *Gentiles*. Not only must the Jewish nation hear the gospel, but so also must the Gentile nations. Jesus warned his disciples

The responsibility of the Christian disciple is to remain faithful to the testimony of Jesus Christ despite opposition.

not to be fooled by false Christs or to be surprised when various events occurred, because "the end is still to come" (13:7).

While answering these questions, Jesus pointed out that the events he was describing would occur in this generation and that the disciples must be prepared to face opposition, suffering, and even death while remaining faithful to him and his teachings.

When the Roman emperor Constantine declared Christianity to be the religion of the state in the fourth century A.D., Christians went from being a persecuted minority to a favored majority. However, through the centuries and in different settings, Christians have continued to face opposition, suffering, and death for their faith. Some face opposition, suffering, and death from governments. Others face opposition, suffering, and death from the community or even their own family members.

> . . . A religion that gives nothing, costs nothing, and suffers nothing is worth nothing.

Faithful in the Face of Opposition

Jesus warned his disciples that they would face opposition from people they had never met and opposition from people in their own family (13:9, 11, 12–13). Who were these people who would oppose the disciples of Jesus Christ, and why would they oppose them? Jewish leaders opposed the disciples because the disciples believed Jesus was the Christ and worshiped him as the true God. Proclaiming this belief would cause them to be delivered to the "local councils" and "synagogues." The Roman occupiers opposed the disciples, blaming Christians for their national troubles. Many Roman citizens claimed that ignoring their household gods to follow Jesus had brought on these problems. These citizens put pressure on governmental authorities, who then began opposing Christians.

Being faithful to Jesus Christ is the most serious commitment of life.

Where does opposition to Christian discipleship arise from today? Who are the ones who oppose the witness of Christ? Opposition includes the opposition of authorities, the opposition of culture, the opposition of other religions, and the opposition of family. Even though freedom of religion is guaranteed by the First Amendment to the United States Constitution, opposition can arise from the interpretation of certain laws or through certain policies or practices. Cultural beliefs and values often run counter to Christian beliefs and values. Some authoritarian religions oppose the Christian faith very strongly. Finally, some Christians face strong opposition to their faith from within their own family. A non-Christian family member can harass and persecute Christian members in many ways, such as ridiculing them or forbidding them to attend worship or to read the Bible.

How does one remain faithful in the face of these kinds of opposition? Jesus told his disciples not to worry about what to say, specifically when they were "arrested and brought to trial" (13:11). Peter and John faced opposition, and God spoke through them (Acts 4:7–12). Stephen and Paul faced opposition, and God spoke through them (Acts 7; 24:10–26).

The provision of God in what to say during times of opposition certainly is not intended to encourage spiritual laziness. Paul reminded Timothy, "All Scripture is God-breathed and is useful for teaching, rebuking, correcting and training in righteousness, so that the man of God may be thoroughly equipped for every good work" (2 Timothy 3:16–17). Peter reminded his readers, "Always be prepared to give an answer to everyone who asks you to give the reason for the hope that you have" (1 Peter 3:15). God will provide the recall for those who need it during times of opposition. God also will provide the power of the Holy Spirit to enable us to maintain a faithful Christian witness.

> To be faithful to Jesus Christ, we must be willing to live an exemplary Christian life and on every occasion to present a clear witness for the hope that is within us.

The responsibility of the Christian disciple is to remain faithful to the testimony of Jesus Christ despite opposition. Jesus said, "If they persecuted me, they will persecute you also" (John 15:20).

Faithful in the Face of Suffering

The opposition Jesus described would become violent for some of his disciples. It would involve suffering. Jesus promised that his disciples would be "flogged in the synagogues" because of their faithful witness about him. We see this demonstrated clearly in the witness of Paul described in 2 Corinthians 11:23–28.

Jesus also promised there would be "days of distress unequaled from the beginning, when God created the world, until now—and never to be equaled again" (Mark 13:19). Suffering accompanying the fall of Jerusalem and the destruction of the temple in 70 A.D. is described by the Jewish historian Josephus as a horror that defied words to express. Jesus said, "If the Lord had not cut short those days, no one would survive" (13:20). Following a long siege, Jerusalem fell into horrific suffering, but it was soon over.

How does a Christian remain faithful in the face of suffering? Certainly there must be some reasonable explanation for not giving up one's faith in the face of suffering. The Scriptures give us some wonderful reasons for holding onto our faith in the face of suffering. The Apostle Paul wrote that not only should we remain faithful to the witness of Christ in our suffering, but also we should rejoice in our sufferings because "suffering produces perseverance; perseverance, character; and character, hope" (Romans 5:3–5). Many faithful Christians have found great value in suffering for the faith. It has been said that a religion that gives nothing, costs nothing, and suffers nothing is worth nothing.

Several years ago, while working on a mission project in Mexico, I bought several clay flower pots to take home to my wife. She was so proud of those pots. We planted several beautiful plants in them and watched them begin to grow. I faithfully watered them every week. Several months later I came out to water the plants and found the pots had fallen apart. They were in a big heap of clay. They evidently had not been in a kiln to make them strong. So it is with our faith. Suffering has a way of firing our faith so that it doesn't crumble.

> *When a believer suffers for his or her faith, that believer is following the example set by Jesus Christ (1 Pet. 2:21).*

The Scriptures also teach that it is "commendable" to bear unjust suffering (1 Peter 2:19). When a believer suffers for his or her faith, that believer is following the example set by Jesus Christ (1 Pet. 2:21). Some preachers portray Christianity as a way to avoid suffering. God is presented as a great spiritual Santa Claus who lives to give everything to his children and spare them from all suffering. This is opposite to what the Scriptures teach.

Peter wrote that when we suffer as a Christian we should not be ashamed but thankful that we bear the name of Christ (1 Pet. 4:16). Paul invited Timothy to join with him in "suffering for the gospel"

(2 Timothy 1:8). Being faithful in the face of suffering links us with other believers who have followed the example of Jesus Christ and have thus built Christian character with great hope.

Faithful in the Face of Death

A pastor told of finding that the man who decreed that women must wear hats in church suffered a martyr's death. He said, "I do not find that surprising. The last time I made any wardrobe suggestions to my wife and two daughters, I almost suffered the same fate."

Martyrdom was a reality in the early church, and it didn't occur because of wardrobe suggestions. Faithfulness to Jesus Christ would mean death for some of his followers (13:12), but the one who "stands firm to the end will be saved" (Mark 13:13). The end would be the end of one's life or the end of time, whichever came first. The phrase "stands firm" renders one Greek word that means *to remain under a load until arriving at the destination*. The verb translated "will be saved" in most instances refers to spiritual salvation, but it must be translated in context. The Scriptures teach that our salvation is a finished fact. It is by grace through faith and not by works (Ephesians 2:8–9). Therefore, in this context, Jesus was not saying that faithfulness until death provides salvation, but rather he was saying that those who carry their commitment (*load*) to him all the way to the end will experience the full measure of the salvation he has provided. The follower of Christ is to be prepared and constantly ready for the end since the time of "that day and hour" (13:32–37) is not known by human beings.

The first-century disciples faced death every day because of their consistent witness to their faith in Jesus Christ (Rom. 8:36) They were able to face death because Jesus removed the sting (1 Cor. 15:55) and the power (Revelation 20:6) of death through his own death on the cross.

For a person to seek to avoid death is natural. Anthropologists tell us that the highest law of nature is self-preservation. People ordinarily will attempt to save their lives in any circumstance. The ultimate price to pay is to give one's life for another person or cause.

Some psychologists say that the fears of rejection, abandonment, failure, separation, and loss are really manifestations of our one ultimate fear—the fear of death. How do we overcome that ultimate fear? We overcome it by faith in the God who overcame it in the resurrection of Jesus Christ. Jesus said in John 11:25–26, "I am the resurrection and the life. He who believes in me will live, even though he dies, and whoever lives and believes in me will never die."

Even though Christians in America rarely face death for their faith, Christians in other parts of the world face death regularly for their faith. These are the ones most closely linked to the Christian martyrs of the first three centuries. These are the ones who are learning what it means to follow Christ even to their death.

As an elderly pastor lay dying, one of his deacons asked him if he was afraid of crossing over the river of death. "Why?" replied the elderly pastor, "I belong to a Father who owns the land on both sides of the river." Being faithful in the face of death requires a confidence in a heavenly Father who owns the land on both sides of the river.

Applying This Lesson to Life

Being faithful to Jesus Christ is the most serious commitment of life. Most believers in the Western world do not have the worries of suffering and death because of their faith. But they do face opposition on many levels. A Western culture dominated by celebrity heroes often presents an immoral or amoral standard of life. Rampant materialism invites one to ignore the demands of the gospel and to live a selfish and self-centered life.

To be faithful to Jesus Christ, we must be willing to live an exemplary Christian life and on every occasion to present a clear witness for the hope that is within us. This requires us to be familiar with the Scriptures and to be disciplined in our daily activities. It also requires us to be willing to live sacrificially so we can extend Christian hospitality to those in need.

When? What Should I Do?

The destruction of the temple in Jerusalem would be a cataclysmic event for the Jews, including Jesus' disciples. This event would take place during "this generation" (Mark 13:30). People would flee from Jerusalem to escape the destruction. But the end of time would not be yet (13:7). In fact, says verse 7, "the end is still to come." Verses 32 states, "No one knows about that day or hour, not even the angels in heaven, nor the Son, but only the Father."

The end of time began with the coming of Jesus Christ. His birth began the last days (Hebrews 1:2). We know that we are living in the end times, but only God knows the end of the end. We are not required to know the dates. Rather, we are to "be on guard! Be alert!" (13:33). The meaning of these two imperatives is: *Live a consistent Christian life at all times because the end of time is not the end of existence.*

Case Study

Betsy Smith was a talented young musician who had excelled at every level of competition. As a junior in high school, she was living her dream of being one of the star performers. She had a strong possibility of getting a four-year scholarship to a major university.

Lesson 11: Discipleship in Dangerous Times

Betsy knew that having a paid education would help her family a great deal. There was only one catch. In order to continue in her coveted position and have a chance for a scholarship, Betsy would have to go to practice on Sunday mornings. This meant missing Bible study and worship. Her band director made it clear that only those who were willing to give this extra effort would maintain their position and be recommended for a scholarship. How would you counsel Betsy?

Questions

1. What is one example of facing opposition to your personal Christian faith?

2. How have you suffered for your Christian faith?

3. How should we respond to the threat of death for witnessing about Jesus?

4. How can you assist those who are suffering and dying for their faith?

Main Idea

We are to live in complete faithfulness to Jesus, remembering that he gave his life for us.

Question to Explore

How can we avoid failing to be faithful to Jesus?

LESSON TWELVE

Not Me

Study Aim

To explain the significance of the Lord's Supper and to state how it encourages faithful discipleship

Study and Action Emphases

- Affirm the Bible as our authoritative guide for life and ministry
- Share the gospel with all people
- Develop a growing, vibrant faith
- Equip people for servant leadership

Quick Read

The events of the Passover meal remind believers of the difficulty of being faithful to Jesus. The best motivation for being faithful to Jesus is to remember that Jesus gave his body and blood to establish a new agreement between God and humankind.

Our church serves the Lord's Supper in the homes of members who are unable to attend the regular services. Several deacons go along with me to visit, read Scripture, sing, pray, and serve the Lord's Supper.

Most of the members we visit in this way are older. They have been believers for years and have served faithfully. Now, though, they are unable to do so because of age or health. But in every case they have a story to tell. They never fail to share how grateful they are for the grace and forgiveness of God through the death and resurrection of Jesus. These are very emotional events for each of us as we share the Lord's Supper and remember together what Jesus did for us by giving his body and blood to provide us with salvation. We are also reminded through the lives of these older believers of our commitment to be faithful to Jesus to the very end of life.

Mark 14:10–31

¹⁰Then Judas Iscariot, one of the Twelve, went to the chief priests to betray Jesus to them. ¹¹They were delighted to hear this and promised to give him money. So he watched for an opportunity to hand him over.

¹²On the first day of the Feast of Unleavened Bread, when it was customary to sacrifice the Passover lamb, Jesus' disciples asked him, "Where do you want us to go and make preparations for you to eat the Passover?"

13So he sent two of his disciples, telling them, "Go into the city, and a man carrying a jar of water will meet you. Follow him. **14**Say to the owner of the house he enters, 'The Teacher asks: Where is my guest room, where I may eat the Passover with my disciples?' **15**He will show you a large upper room, furnished and ready. Make preparations for us there."

16The disciples left, went into the city and found things just as Jesus had told them. So they prepared the Passover.

17When evening came, Jesus arrived with the Twelve. **18**While they were reclining at the table eating, he said, "I tell you the truth, one of you will betray me—one who is eating with me."

19They were saddened, and one by one they said to him, "Surely not I?"

20"It is one of the Twelve," he replied, "one who dips bread into the bowl with me. **21**The Son of Man will go just as it is written about him. But woe to that man who betrays the Son of Man! It would be better for him if he had not been born."

22While they were eating, Jesus took bread, gave thanks and broke it, and gave it to his disciples, saying, "Take it; this is my body."

23Then he took the cup, gave thanks and offered it to them, and they all drank from it.

24"This is my blood of the covenant, which is poured out for many," he said to them. **25**"I tell you the truth, I will not drink again of the fruit of the vine until that day when I drink it anew in the kingdom of God."

26When they had sung a hymn, they went out to the Mount of Olives.

27"You will all fall away," Jesus told them, "for it is written:

"'I will strike the shepherd,
and the sheep will be scattered.'

28But after I have risen, I will go ahead of you into Galilee."

29Peter declared, "Even if all fall away, I will not."

30"I tell you the truth," Jesus answered, "today—yes, tonight—before the rooster crows twice you yourself will disown me three times."

31But Peter insisted emphatically, "Even if I have to die with you, I will never disown you." And all the others said the same.

Faithfulness in the Midst of Materialism (14:1–11)

One of the last prophetic ministries extended to Jesus before the Passover Supper was that of the woman who anointed Jesus with perfume (Mark 14:1–9). Although the disciples protested about the extravagance of this beautiful and simple action, Jesus commended the woman for doing "what she could" (14:8). Even though it was a simple act, it had profound implications. Jesus noted that what she did was a prophetic statement about his coming death. He also reminded the disciples that this woman, by her actions, would take her place in redemptive history wherever the gospel was preached. The record of this simple act should remind every Christian of the power resident within what many might consider everyday acts of kindness in the name of Jesus.

It is ironic that as a disciple of Jesus Christ, Judas would be so ignorant of the prophetic significance of this action (14:10–11). Instead of being grateful for this woman's offering and its importance in signaling the redemptive death of Jesus Christ, Judas immediately made an agreement to betray Jesus for a sum of money.

Why would Judas betray Jesus for money? Mark writes that some of the disciples protested the waste of money by this woman (14:4), indicating that the money could have been given to the poor. The Gospel of John implicates Judas in this protest. It states that Judas was not interested in the poor but in his own

Materialism is a real and prevalent threat to faithful discipleship.

selfish greed; he was a thief who regularly stole from the money bag (John 12:4–6). Therefore, it appears that Judas's motive for betraying Jesus was financial gain, which would have been consistent with his nature. Paul reminded Timothy, "For the love of money is a root of all kinds of evil. Some people, eager for money, have wandered from the faith and pierced themselves with many griefs" (1 Timothy 6:10).

Materialism is a real and prevalent threat to faithful discipleship. In many ways, both large and small, materialism crowds out time and energy that should be devoted to following Jesus faithfully. Prosperity often opens opportunities that individuals and families have never had before. They can travel more, participate in more activities, shop more, and generally enjoy the material side of life more. Unfortunately, these good opportunities can draw people away from the best opportunities to worship and serve Jesus Christ.

Money and materialism empower people in ways that are deceptive and destructive. Much like the rich farmer mentioned by Jesus in Luke 12:18–21, people begin to trust in their wealth and forget to be rich toward God. Their money gives them a sense of power that makes them imagine they can buy everything they need to make them secure and happy. But like the Prodigal Son of Luke 15, one day they find themselves in a far country needing to return to the Father's house.

> *Materialism and greed can cause one to be unfaithful to Jesus, leading to a life filled with remorse and tragedy.*

Judas would be "seized with remorse" when he saw what his greed had done to Jesus and the relationship they once enjoyed, but it would be too late to save Jesus' life (Matthew 27:3–5). Materialism and greed can cause one to be unfaithful to Jesus, leading to a life filled with remorse and tragedy.

Jesus made it very clear that having things is okay and necessary but that having things should come second to having a vital trust in him (Matt. 6:32–33).

We must remain faithful to Jesus Christ in the midst of the temptations of materialism.

Faithfulness in the Face of Fear (14:12–21, 27–31)

The Jewish people were coming to Jerusalem to celebrate the Feast of Unleavened Bread and the sacrifice of the Passover lamb. They would recall the events that led them from slavery in Egypt to freedom in the Promised Land. Exodus 12 gives the details of the Passover. Unleavened bread was to be prepared, indicating the swiftness of the escape from Egypt. A lamb was to be slain and the blood placed on the doorpost of each Jewish home so that the death angel would pass over that home and not take the firstborn. This celebration was to be a "last-ing ordinance for the generations to come" (Exodus 12:17). This observance celebrated the freedom God had given the people of Israel from their slavery in Egypt.

The sacrificial death of Jesus Christ, represented by Jesus in the bread and the wine of the Passover meal, reminds every believer of the price paid for his or her salvation.

Jesus and his disciples made preparations for celebrating this "lasting ordinance" by finding "a large upper room, furnished and ready" (Mark 14:15). In this room during the meal, Jesus would reveal the shocking truth that one of the disciples would betray him. The disciples were saddened that Jesus would infer that one of them would betray him. They began to ask (14:19), "Surely not I?"

Later, Jesus would again assert that he would be forsaken, not by the betrayal of just one, but by the falling away of all (14:27). He said this in the context of his coming death on the cross (14:8–9). At this point, Peter boldly declared, "Even if all fall away, I will not" (14:29). Jesus confronted Peter's denial by saying pointedly, "Tonight— before the rooster crows twice you yourself will disown me three times" (14:30). Peter responded even more boldly, "Even if I have to die with you, I will never disown you." In fact, "all the others said the same" (14:31). At this point, not one of the disciples could admit that he would ever be so afraid that he would be unfaithful to Jesus.

Taking the Lord's Supper together encourages every believer to be faithful to Jesus Christ, who graciously took our sins upon himself so that we could be completely forgiven and cleansed of all unrighteousness.

In the face of Jesus' arrest and condemnation to death, Peter's fear overcame his earlier commitments to faithfulness (see 14:66–72). The crowing of the rooster reminded Peter of his earlier promises to Jesus, and Peter "broke down and wept" (14:72).

Paul gave a strong warning in 1 Corinthians 10:12, "So, if you think you are standing firm, be careful that you don't fall!" Peter and all the other disciples thought they were standing firm, but when they saw that Jesus was arrested and condemned to death, their fear caused them to abandon him.

Each one of us will confront the temptation to be unfaithful to Jesus in the face of our fears. Sometimes we take counsel in our fears instead of in our faith, and we decide that distancing ourselves from our faith is the safest thing to do. Sometimes people abandon Jesus in order to maintain their popularity with faithless people. Others abandon Jesus for fear of not getting ahead in life. Still others abandon Jesus for fear being faithful will cost them too much. Much of the lying, cheating, and stealing done in our world is done by those who at one time expressed an undying faith in Jesus Christ. Why do they do it? It is often out of fear of not getting what they want or not getting to where they want to be in life.

Jesus' death on the cross paid a price we could not pay for a gift we could never earn.

Believers are called to be faithful even in the face of suffering and death. Paul wrote in Philippians 1:20–21, "I eagerly expect and hope that I will in no way be ashamed, but will have sufficient courage so that now as always Christ will be exalted in my body, whether by life or by death. For to me to live is Christ and to die is gain." Had these disciples grasped the truth of Jesus' words when he said (Mark 14:28), "But after I have risen, I will go ahead of you into Galilee," they would have realized that for the believer death is not the final word. No doubt their faith would have been stronger and their denials would have been unnecessary if they had relied on Jesus' promise that he would rise from the grave and meet them again in Galilee.

Faithfulness in the Gift of Grace (14:22–26)

After revealing that one of the disciples would betray him, Jesus shifted the conversation to the significance of his coming death. He used the common elements of bread and wine to illustrate the price being paid for the new agreement God was making with humankind. Jesus used the bread as a symbol of his body, which would be given in sacrifice for humankind's sin. Jesus had used bread to feed multitudes on two occasions (6:35–42; 8:1–13; see also 8:14–21). Bread was a basic food and was used by Jesus as a metaphor for spiritual and supernatural food. He referred to himself as "the bread of life" (John 6:35). Jesus wanted his disciples to understand that taking the bread was symbolic of taking on themselves faith in his death on their behalf, something they did not yet understand fully.

Jesus' body and blood were given to establish a new agreement between God and humankind.

Next Jesus "took the cup, gave thanks, and offered it" to his disciples so that each could drink from it (Mark 14:23). He described the cup as "my blood of the covenant, which is poured out for many" (14:24)

202

Earlier in the Gospel of Mark, Jesus had used the symbol of the cup to point to his death (10:38–39).

In the Gospel of Luke and in some manuscripts of the Gospels of Matthew and Mark, this covenant is described as a "new" covenant (Matt. 26:28; Mark 14:24; Luke 22:20). The former covenant between God and humankind was based on faithfulness to the Old Testament law, with animal sacrifices offered as atonement for breaking the law. Jesus' own death would replace animal sacrifices as the atonement God would require. The new covenant established a relationship between God and humankind resting on love rather than law. This relationship was based on God's grace in Jesus Christ.

Jesus then told his disciples that he would "not drink of the fruit of the vine until that day when I drink it anew in the kingdom of God" (Mark 14:25). In Jewish thought, heaven would be a great banquet with a sumptuous feast to eat and wine to drink (Luke 22:30). The celebration of the Lord's Supper is not only a time to remember what Jesus has done for us but also a time to look forward to Jesus' return when there will be a resurrection of the body and a glorious reward in heaven (1 Cor. 11:26).

The sacrificial death of Jesus Christ, represented by Jesus in the bread and the wine of the Passover meal, reminds every believer of the price paid for his or her salvation. Each time the Lord's Supper is served we are again confronted with this gracious and loving sacrifice for our sins. Taking the Lord's

Supper together encourages every believer to be faithful to Jesus Christ, who graciously took our sins upon himself so that we could be completely forgiven and cleansed of all unrighteousness. As Paul wrote, "God made him who had no sin to be sin for us, so that in him we might become the righteousness of God" (2 Corinthians 5:21).

Implications and Actions

Jesus' death on the cross paid a price we could not pay for a gift we could never earn. Jesus' body and blood were given to establish a new agreement between God and humankind. The writer of Hebrews tells us that Jesus set aside the first covenant, a covenant of law, to establish the second, a covenant of grace (see Hebrews 10:9–10).

Jesus' Blood

Jesus' reference to the cup as his "blood" (Mark 14:24) would have been repulsive to faithful Jews. Their own Scriptures forbade them eating any blood: "Any Israelite or any alien living among them who eats any blood—I will set my face against that person who eats blood and will cut him off from his people. For the life of a creature is in the blood, and I have given it to you to make atonement for yourselves on the altar; it is the blood that makes atonement for one's life" (Leviticus 17:10–11).

The disciples had been reared to observe the strict teachings of the *Torah* (the first five books of the Bible). They would have been familiar with the Scriptures forbidding them from drinking literal blood. They would have understood the symbolic nature of Jesus' words, "This is my blood of the covenant, which is poured out for many" (Mark 14:24).

Case Study

A young man named Tom attended a church that served the Lord's Supper every Sunday. One weekend he attended a football game in another city and stayed over on Sunday. When he woke up on Sunday morning, he asked his friends where he could find a church like his home church. His friends didn't know where one was located but invited him to attend a nearby church with them. He became very upset and told them that he had to attend a church like his and take the Lord's Supper because doing so was crucial to his salvation. How would you have addressed that belief?

Questions

1. In what areas of life are you most tempted to betray Jesus?

2. What example can you cite in which someone—perhaps you—remained faithful to Jesus in spite of great temptation or fear?

3. Why do Baptists believe that when taking the Lord's Supper, the bread and wine are symbolic of Jesus' body and blood?

4. What experiences of the Lord's Supper have been most helpful in encouraging you to more faithful discipleship?

Focal Text

Mark 14:61b–64; 15:9–24, 37–41; 16:1–8

Background

Mark 14:32—16:8

Main Idea

We can trust in and follow Jesus as the crucified yet victorious Son of God because of his resurrection.

Question to Explore

How does Jesus' crucifixion and resurrection affect your life?

LESSON THIRTEEN

The Worst and Best of Times

Study Aim

To affirm or re-affirm my trust in Jesus as the crucified yet victorious Son of God

Study and Action Emphases

- Affirm the Bible as our authoritative guide for life and ministry
- Share the gospel with all people
- Develop a growing, vibrant faith
- Equip people for servant leadership

Quick Read

Jesus was betrayed, condemned, mocked, beaten, and crucified. Then came the wonderful news (Mark 16:6), "He has risen!"

Several years ago I had the privilege of baptizing a young girl named Anastasia. She was thrilled when I told the congregation that this young girl's English name was taken from the Greek word *anastasis*, which means *to stand again, to stand up again,* or *to rise again.* Thus, this Greek word is the word for *resurrection.* The resurrection of Jesus reminds us that even though we lie down in death, we will stand again in life. Young Anastasia's baptism was a graphic illustration of the truth of Jesus' resurrection and the promise of our own resurrection.

What does the crucifixion and resurrection of Jesus Christ in the first century have to do with our lives in the twenty-first century? Let us look for the answer as we study the Scriptures for this lesson.

Mark 14:61b–64

Again the high priest asked him, "Are you the Christ, the Son of the Blessed One?"

62"I am," said Jesus. "And you will see the Son of Man sitting at the right hand of the Mighty One and coming on the clouds of heaven."

63The high priest tore his clothes. "Why do we need any more witnesses?" he asked. 64"You have heard the blasphemy. What do you think?"

They all condemned him as worthy of death.

Mark 15:9–24, 37–41

9"Do you want me to release to you the king of the Jews?" asked Pilate, **10**knowing it was out of envy that the chief priests had handed Jesus over to him. **11**But the chief priests stirred up the crowd to have Pilate release Barabbas instead.

12"What shall I do, then, with the one you call the king of the Jews?" Pilate asked them.

13"Crucify him!" they shouted.

14"Why? What crime has he committed?" asked Pilate.

But they shouted all the louder, "Crucify him!"

15Wanting to satisfy the crowd, Pilate released Barabbas to them. He had Jesus flogged, and handed him over to be crucified.

16The soldiers led Jesus away into the palace (that is, the Praetorium) and called together the whole company of soldiers. **17**They put a purple robe on him, then twisted together a crown of thorns and set it on him. **18**And they began to call out to him, "Hail, king of the Jews!" **19**Again and again they struck him on the head with a staff and spit on him. Falling on their knees, they paid homage to him. **20**And when they had mocked him, they took off the purple robe and put his own clothes on him. Then they led him out to crucify him.

21A certain man from Cyrene, Simon, the father of Alexander and Rufus, was passing by on his way in from the country, and they forced him to carry the cross.

THE GOSPEL OF MARK: *Jesus' Works and Words*

22They brought Jesus to the place called Golgotha (which means The Place of the Skull). **23**Then they offered him wine mixed with myrrh, but he did not take it. **24**And they crucified him. Dividing up his clothes, they cast lots to see what each would get.

• • • • • • • • • • • • • • • • • • • •

37With a loud cry, Jesus breathed his last.

38The curtain of the temple was torn in two from top to bottom. **39**And when the centurion, who stood there in front of Jesus, heard his cry and saw how he died, he said, "Surely this man was the Son of God!"

40Some women were watching from a distance. Among them were Mary Magdalene, Mary the mother of James the younger and of Joses, and Salome. **41**In Galilee these women had followed him and cared for his needs. Many other women who had come up with him to Jerusalem were also there.

Mark 16:1–8

1When the Sabbath was over, Mary Magdalene, Mary the mother of James, and Salome bought spices so that they might go to anoint Jesus' body. **2**Very early on the first day of the week, just after sunrise, they were on their way to the tomb **3**and they asked each other, "Who will roll the stone away from the entrance of the tomb?"

4But when they looked up, they saw that the stone, which was very large, had been rolled away. **5**As they entered the tomb, they saw a young man dressed in a white robe sitting on the right side, and they were alarmed.

6"Don't be alarmed," he said. "You are looking for Jesus the Nazarene, who was crucified. He has risen! He is not here. See the place where they laid him. **7**But go, tell his disciples and Peter, 'He is going ahead of you into Galilee. There you will see him, just as he told you.'"

8Trembling and bewildered, the women went out and fled from the tomb. They said nothing to anyone, because they were afraid.

Background and Overview of the Events

As Jesus moved toward the time of his arrest and crucifixion, he took his disciples to the Garden of Gethsemane so that they could keep watch for him while he prayed (Mark 14:32–42). Jesus agonized in prayer over God's will for him to die for the sins of the world. His agony was compounded by his own disciples' inability or unwillingness to stay awake while he prayed.

Suddenly Judas, the betrayer, appeared (14:43–49). He brought with him an armed mob. Judas kissed Jesus on the cheek to identify him so that the soldiers could arrest the right person. In a burst of irony, Jesus asked why a mob was brought to arrest him since these people should recognize him from the times he had taught in the temple courts. He then reminded them that this kind of arrest would simply fulfill the Scriptures.

Following his arrest, everyone deserted Jesus, including one young man who fled naked, leaving his garment behind (14:50–52). Some scholars suggest that the young man who fled naked was none other than Mark, the author of this Gospel.

The resurrection of Jesus reminds us that even though we lie down in death, we will stand again in life.

The various groups referred to in 14:53 comprised the Sanhedrin, the supreme court of the Jews. So Jesus was taken to face the high priest and the entire Sanhedrin. After listening to false testimony about Jesus, the high priest asked Jesus (14:61), "Are you the Christ, the Son of the Blessed One?" "'I am,' said Jesus" (14:62).

When Jesus admitted he was the Christ, the high priest flew into a rage, accusing Jesus of blasphemy, condemning him to death. The other members of the Sanhedrin joined in this condemnation. Jesus was blindfolded, and people began to spit on him and beat him as he was led away (14:63–65).

Meanwhile, a servant girl recognized Peter and accused him of being with Jesus, an accusation that Peter quickly and adamantly denied three times. When Peter heard the cock crow the second time, he remembered the words of Jesus. He broke down and wept (14:66–72).

Jesus was bound over and taken to face the Roman governor, Pilate. When Pilate asked whether Jesus was the king of the Jews, Jesus replied that he was. After further accusations by the chief priests, Pilate attempted to have Jesus released, but the crowd chose Barabbas (15:1–14). "Wanting to satisfy the crowd, Pilate released Barabbas to them. He had Jesus flogged, and handed him over to be crucified" (15:15).

Jesus' example of courage and faithfulness in the face of conflict gives us courage and faith to face our conflicts.

After Jesus was crucified, Pilate released the body to Joseph of Arimathea for burial. Joseph was a prominent member of the Sanhedrin. He took Jesus' body, put it into a tomb, and rolled a stone across the entrance (15:42–47).

Courage in the Face of Conflict

The story is told of a young soldier fighting in Italy during World War II, who jumped into a foxhole to avoid being shot. He immediately tried to deepen the hole for more protection and was frantically scraping dirt with his hands. He unearthed something metal and brought up a silver crucifix, left by a former resident of the foxhole. A moment later another leaping figure landed beside him as the shells screamed overhead. When the soldier got a chance to look, he saw that his new companion was an army chaplain.

215

Holding out the crucifix, the soldier gasped, "Am I glad to see you! How do you work this thing?"

Probably each one of us has times in life when we want to know how to work this thing called faith! How does one continue to follow God in the face of serious conflict and suffering?

Jesus' ability to see into the future made him acutely aware of the suffering he faced on the way to the cross. The Gospel of Mark recorded this prediction in 8:31; 9:31; and 10:33–34. Jesus said he would be betrayed, and it happened just as he said (14:10–52). Jesus said he would be condemned to death, and it happened just as he said (14:53–65). Jesus said he would be handed over to the Gentiles, and it happened just as he said (15:1–20). Jesus said he would be mocked, scourged, and killed by the Gentiles, and it happened just as he said (15:21–47). Jesus said he would be raised three days later, and it happened just as he said (16:1–8). At any point along this path, Jesus could have changed his mind. Instead, he willingly walked this road of conflict and suffering in order to do the will of God.

They knew that earthly death was but a transition to eternal life.

Jesus' example of courage and faithfulness in the face of conflict gives us courage and faith to face our conflicts. He knew that doing what is right brings the right result, even if there is conflict and suffering in the interim.

Conflict and suffering were no surprise to Jesus as he made his way to the cross. Neither should conflict and suffering be a surprise to us when we are doing God's will. Jesus said, "I have told you these things, so that in me you may have peace. In this world you will have trouble. But take heart! I have overcome the world" (John 16:33). Trouble is part of being in the world and being opposed by the godless world system.

Note that Jesus gave prominence to women during his ministry and inspired in them a faith that persevered in the face of suffering and death.

The crucifixion and resurrection of Jesus should give us courage to move through the fires of conflict and suffering that come to all who faithfully follow Jesus. The writer of Hebrews encourages us in the face of suffering by saying,

> Let us fix our eyes on Jesus, the author and perfecter of our faith, who for the joy set before him endured the cross, scorning its shame, and sat down at the right hand of the throne of God. Consider him who endured such opposition from sinful men, so that you will not grow weary and lose heart (Hebrews 12:2–3).

Confidence in the Face of Death

The crucifixion and resurrection of Jesus remind us that sin brought about humankind's death, but Jesus' death brought about humankind's forgiveness and eternal life. Paul wrote, "The sting of death is sin, and the power of sin is in the law. But thanks be to God! He gives us the victory through our Lord Jesus Christ" (1 Corinthians 15:56–57).

All people face death. We don't know when or how we will die, but we know that we will die. Death has its terrors. Death is a passing from all that is familiar to that which is new and unfamiliar. But believers in Jesus Christ can face death with confidence. Peter wrote, "Through him you believe in God, who raised him from the dead and glorified him, and so your faith and hope are in God" (1 Peter 1:21).

The resurrection of Jesus Christ gives us the opportunity to know him personally, not to just know about him.

Jesus' death saddened and discouraged his followers, and his resurrection scared and bewildered them. When the women who came to Jesus' tomb were told, "He has risen! He is not here" (Mark 16:6), they weren't prepared to deal with his resurrection. Matthew adds that the women were "afraid yet filled with joy" (Matthew 28:8).

Even though the women and the disciples were at first scared and incredulous in the face of the resurrection, they were soon transformed by it. Simon

Peter, James, and John became forceful preachers of the gospel after seeing the resurrected Jesus. Members of the early church suffered and died for their faith in the resurrected Jesus. They knew that earthly death was but a transition to eternal life. They had witnessed it in the crucifixion and resurrection of Jesus.

As twenty-first century believers, we can place our faith in the reality of Paul's assertion in Colossians 2:13–15,

> When you were dead in your sins and in the uncircumcision of your sinful nature, God made you alive with Christ. He forgave us all our sins, having canceled the written code, with its regulations, that was against us and that stood opposed to us; he took it away, nailing it to the cross. And having disarmed the powers and authorities, he made a public spectacle of them, triumphing over them by the cross.

Through the resurrection of Jesus Christ, we have been made alive through the forgiveness of our sins and the indwelling of the Holy Spirit. Our death will not be the end of all endings but the beginning of all beginnings.

Confirmation in the Face of the Resurrection

"Mary Magdalene, Mary the mother of James the younger and of Joses, and Salome" had been faithful to stay with Jesus while he was being crucified (Mark 15:40). "Many other women who had come up with him to Jerusalem were also there" (15:41). They had maintained a loving vigil despite the cruelties and suffering of the cross. They had remained faithful in the face of persecution by the religious and political authorities. They had not deserted Jesus. They had begun this ministry with Jesus in Galilee, and they were with Jesus at the very end.

Jesus' example of faithfulness to God's task for him inspires us to remain faithful to all God expects of us.

Not only were these women faithful to Jesus during his suffering and death, but they also were the first ones to visit his tomb following his burial, "when the Sabbath was over" (16:1). Jesus' resurrection was confirmed to these faithful women. They were given instructions to go and tell his disciples including Peter (16:7). Peter perhaps was singled out because he was the one who seemed most distraught at his own weakness and denial of Jesus. Peter was singled out to hear clearly that his betrayal of Jesus was not the end. Jesus had another word for Peter, and it was the word of forgiveness and grace—the result of the cross and the resurrection.

Jesus would indeed meet his disciples in Galilee, just as he had predicted in Mark 14:28. He met Simon Peter, Thomas, Nathanael, the sons of Zebedee, and two other disciples on the shore of the Sea of

Tiberias. There Jesus restored Simon Peter and commissioned him for further service (John 21).

Note that Jesus gave prominence to women during his ministry and inspired in them a faith that persevered in the face of suffering and death. He did not discriminate against them because of their gender, which was done regularly in the first-century Jewish world. God first announced the resurrection to these women, and God entrusted to them the privilege of passing on the information of this revolutionary event. God rewarded their faith and their perseverance.

> In Jesus' resurrection, we find not only victory over death but grace in time of suffering.

The resurrection of Jesus Christ gives us the opportunity to know him personally, not to just know about him. We may know *about* great historical personalities, but we can know Jesus through a personal relationship with him. Such a relationship would not have been possible without Jesus' resurrection. Have you met the resurrected Jesus and accepted him as your Lord and Savior?

Implications and Actions

Jesus' example of faithfulness to God's task for him inspires us to remain faithful to all God expects of us.

Jesus knew that suffering and death was the price for humankind's salvation. He also knew that resurrection would be the final outcome. Yet Jesus had to move through the fires of conflict to get to the resurrection.

In Jesus' resurrection, we find not only victory over death but also grace in time of suffering. "Thanks be to God! He gives us the victory through our Lord Jesus Christ" (1 Cor. 15:58).

The Ending of the Gospel of Mark

The earliest and best Greek manuscripts of the Gospel of Mark end at 16:8. Other manuscripts, which are inferior to these manuscripts, add 16:9–20. This additional passage contains some material that is foreign to anything we find in the three other Gospels. Also the style of Greek in verses 9–20 is different from the rest of Mark's Gospel. All of these factors suggest strongly that these verses are not original to the Gospel of Mark. Some scholars suggest that the abrupt ending of Mark's Gospel at verse eight could have been caused by Mark's sudden death, or that perhaps the scroll on which the manuscript was written had that part torn off over the years.

Case Study

A young Christian worked as a mortgage banker in an international banking firm and traveled extensively around the world in many different countries. During this person's first ten years with the firm, he had opportunity to make friends in various countries. Some of these friends were Jewish, and some were Muslim. The banker never felt he had a good opportunity to share the gospel with them until one day when he found himself in a discussion of a recent major airline crash. As he talked with a Jewish friend and a Muslim friend, they wondered aloud about the fate of those on the aircraft. How would you have discussed the possibility of life beyond death with these two friends?

Questions

1. What is an example of a time in your life when you knew doing right would bring suffering but you did right anyway?

2. How can we increase our confidence that there is life beyond death?

3. How can you share your confidence in life beyond the grave with an unbelieving friend?

4. How can you show joy in times of suffering without appearing to be flippant?

5. In what ways can men and women be involved in sharing the good news of Jesus' resurrection?

Main Idea

When we truly understand the meaning of God's sending Jesus, we respond by glorifying and praising God.

Question to Explore

Why does Christ's birth bring such joy?

CHRISTMAS LESSON

Glory to God!

Study Aim

To explain the meaning of God's sending Jesus and respond by glorifying and praising God

Study and Action Emphases

- Affirm the Bible as our authoritative guide for life and ministry
- Share the gospel with all people
- Develop a growing, vibrant faith
- Encourage healthy families
- Obey and serve Jesus by meeting physical, spiritual, and emotional needs

Quick Read

Luke recorded the greatest event in history. The royal birth brought all who saw it to high praise and celebration. A fresh look at the Savior brings outrageous joy today.

Christmas. It's a magical word. It's a word that inspires hope in all of us. Christmas brings joy to every child and makes each of us a child.

Surely we all have a favorite Christmas. For me, it was *the year of the bike*, 1967, I believe. I awoke to the bike of my dreams, just sitting there, wrapped with a bow, under the tree. Then there was 1974, *the year of the tennis racket*. My brother and I each got one. We spent hours on the tennis court that Christmas day, each with his own coveted Wilson T–2000, the most powerful weapon in the world of grass, hard, or clay courts. It was the racket Jimmy Connors used to win multiple U.S. Open titles.

But what we really wanted was snow. In Houston, winter often fell on a Tuesday afternoon. A *snow job* was a failed political promise or a guarantee of a Houston Oiler Super Bowl. We only dreamed of a white Christmas. Thanks to *the Blizzard of 1973*, we always had hope. That was the year of the three-inch snowfall and snowmen that approached six inches in height. The early morning snow stuck to the ground and did not melt until, well, *late* morning.

My favorite Christmas fell in 1975. We were with family in Oklahoma City. It snowed for hours. It was enough fun to make me forget about my favorite gift ever. Even *Rock 'Em, Sock 'Em Robots* could not compete with a foot of snow. The snow was enough to make me forget *the year of the bike, the year of the T–2000*, and every other Christmas past.

Then it happened. They said it was impossible. It had never happened before. On December 25, 2004, millions of Houstonians awoke to five to seven inches of snow. It snowed all the way to the beaches of Galveston. The local weather guys had picked up Santa on the radar but never Christmas snow. It was snowing in Houston, on Christmas Day! My dream had come true. There was just one problem. I wasn't there. Three years earlier, I had given up on my dream and moved to the arctic lands of North Texas. Millions saw it, but I was 300 miles away.

A couple of thousand years ago, a dream was fulfilled in a lowly manger. Isaiah and Micah had dreamed of such a day. But a carpenter got to see it. The king feared it while the angels rejoiced. The CEOs and executives in the downtown skyscrapers of Rome missed it. The manager of the local hotel missed it. But shepherds on the graveyard shift were invited in. They saw the Christ child. They were naturally "terrified," they "hurried" to see him, and they returned to the fields "glorifying and praising God."

Christmas is the word that awakens the child in all of us. Let's take a few minutes and return to the joy and celebration of that first Christmas.

Luke 2:1–20

¹In those days Caesar Augustus issued a decree that a census should be taken of the entire Roman world.

2(This was the first census that took place while Quirinius was governor of Syria.) **3**And everyone went to his own town to register.

4So Joseph also went up from the town of Nazareth in Galilee to Judea, to Bethlehem the town of David, because he belonged to the house and line of David. **5**He went there to register with Mary, who was pledged to be married to him and was expecting a child. **6**While they were there, the time came for the baby to be born, **7**and she gave birth to her firstborn, a son. She wrapped him in cloths and placed him in a manger, because there was no room for them in the inn.

8And there were shepherds living out in the fields nearby, keeping watch over their flocks at night. **9**An angel of the Lord appeared to them, and the glory of the Lord shone around them, and they were terrified. **10**But the angel said to them, "Do not be afraid. I bring you good news of great joy that will be for all the people. **11**Today in the town of David a Savior has been born to you; he is Christ the Lord. **12**This will be a sign to you: You will find a baby wrapped in cloths and lying in a manger."

13Suddenly a great company of the heavenly host appeared with the angel, praising God and saying,

14 "Glory to God in the highest,
and on earth peace to men on whom his favor
rests."

15When the angels had left them and gone into heaven, the shepherds said to one another, "Let's go to

Bethlehem and see this thing that has happened, which the Lord has told us about."

16So they hurried off and found Mary and Joseph, and the baby, who was lying in the manger. **17**When they had seen him, they spread the word concerning what had been told them about this child, **18**and all who heard it were amazed at what the shepherds said to them. **19**But Mary treasured up all these things and pondered them in her heart. **20**The shepherds returned, glorifying and praising God for all the things they had heard and seen, which were just as they had been told.

Praise of Obedience: Joseph and Mary (2:1–7)

It is interesting to watch God interrupt the natural flow of events. The great story began "in those days" (Luke 2:1). Luke was the only Gospel writer to relate the events of Jesus' birth to world history. His Greek audience would be intrigued by such detail. Augustus was the first emperor of Rome, a conqueror who had ended a civil war and brought peace to the land. His reign would last forty-one years, from 27 B.C. to A.D. 14. Augustus, formerly known as Octavian, was renamed and exalted by the Roman Senate. He remains one of very few to have a month named after him (August).

Surely we all have a favorite Christmas.

The contrast between Caesar Augustus, whom they called *savior*, and the true Savior, is striking.

One was born into the home of a prosperous leading family in the great empire, the other into a stable of a common Jewish couple. One came as a conqueror, the other as a servant. One brought worldwide *Pax Romana* (Roman peace); the other gave inner peace. One's birth was likely announced by the Roman Senate, the other's by the shepherds. There is a world of contrast between a king and *the* King.

A "census" was to be taken (2:1). These were conducted every fourteen years. Their purpose was to build the military and collect taxes. Although not bound to military services, the Jews were subject to Roman taxation. "Everyone went to his own town to register" (2:3). They would return to the place where their family records were kept.

Joseph naturally went to Bethlehem, for both he and Mary were descendants of David. It is not clear why Joseph would take Mary. Roman law did not require that she go. (Of course, Mary had to give birth in Bethlehem to fulfill Old Testament prophecy.) Joseph and Mary traveled eighty miles from Nazareth to Bethlehem, in obedience to Roman law and God's plan. The Scriptures had been clear. The Messiah would be born to the house of David (Isaiah 11:1; Jeremiah 33:15).

Christmas is the word that awakens the child in all of us.

The local hotel had a *No Vacancy* sign out front. The innkeeper has gotten a bad rap. Perhaps he did the best he could. The place was full, with many Jewish travelers coming home for the census. Irony abounds. It seems the only place the Roman and Jewish world had for Jesus was a cross. So Joseph brought Mary to the place of a manger. The manger was a feeding trough for animals. They likely filled the trough with a bed of hay. Mary "wrapped him [Jesus] in cloths" (Luke 2:7). Bands of cloth were

God uses and blesses men and women of faithfulness and character.

used to keep the baby warm. A long strip of cloth was wound around a large square cloth, providing a soft cover and protection.

We can respond to the Christ of Christmas in many different ways. The example of Joseph and Mary was one of obedience, to Roman law and God's plan. God surely enjoys the musical celebrations and programs that celebrate the birth of his Son. But the best response is not that of attending such an event but walking in obedience to the Savior.

Praise of Heaven: the Angels (2:8–15)

These verses speak of an "angel," "angels," and a "heavenly host" five times (2:9, 10, 13, 15). "Angel" means *messenger*. The appointed angel first appeared to the shepherds amid a blaze of glory (2:9). His mere appearance understandably "terrified" them (2:9). The night crew had seen a lot as they gazed to the sky—such as falling stars, meteor showers, and lunar eclipses. But this was an angel, an uninvited guest from heaven. The angel's first words were "Do not be afraid," a command found often in the Bible.

The "glory" (2:9) referred to God's majesty and splendor. The messenger then announced "good news . . . for all the people" (2:10), from the rich and famous to the lowly shepherds. The title "Christ the Lord" is found only here in the New Testament (2:11).

"Suddenly a great company of the heavenly host appeared with the angel, praising God" (2:13). "Company" was a military term for a band of soldiers. This band of angels was similar to John's vision of thousands of angels (Revelation 5:11). Their message proclaimed "glory to God" and "peace to men" (Luke 2:15). The angelic host was careful to give glory to the One who set in motion the great events of Christmas.

Whether in ways similar to the quiet obedience of Mary and Joseph, the ecstatic praise of angels, or the outspoken witness of the shepherds, we are to exalt and glorify the Christ of Christmas.

During this Christmas season, we have many ways to praise and glorify our God. Like Joseph and Mary, we may celebrate through quiet obedience to God's plan. We can join with the praises of heaven, announcing Jesus' birth to a fallen world. The holidays offer great opportunities for us to share what the great birth means to us. Nothing would honor the Father more.

Praise Through Witness: the Shepherds (2:16–20)

The story of the shepherds is a four-act play. In act one we find these blue-collar workers faithful at their job. They were "keeping watch over their flocks at night" (2:8). Shepherds were lowly outcasts, not allowed into the city. Their dirty job made it impossible for them to fulfill ceremonial law, for their hands could not be considered clean. It was here, where David had protected his sheep while killing lions and bears, that we find common men doing common work, while being thrust into the greatest story ever told. The lesson is clear. God uses and blesses men and women of faithfulness and character regardless of their social status.

Act two involved a search. When told of the birth, the shepherds did not ask for a sign as Zechariah had (1:18). But the angel told them what to look for, assuming they would naturally search for the child. He would be the one "lying in a manger" (2:12).

The shepherds made a decision. They decided to leave their flocks and go and see the baby (2:15). They made this commitment as a group. "The shepherds said to one another, 'Let's go to Bethlehem and see . . .'" (2:15). They made the decision to risk their job, income, security, and reputation for the chance to meet the Savior. That remains the choice of wisdom today. A better rendering of the text would be, "The shepherds *kept saying* to one another . . ." (italics added for emphasis).

In act three the shepherds acted on their decision. A decision to seek Christ is hollow until we actually seek him. The shepherds sought Jesus with urgency. "They hurried off" (2:16). They saw Jesus personally (2:17). Notice the language of the text. They "found" Mary and Joseph (2:16), but they *saw* Jesus (2:17). The parents got the shepherds' attention, but the Savior won their affection. They glanced at Mary. They acknowledged Joseph. But they gazed at the babe in the manger.

The shepherds' response comprises act four. Amazingly, their first response was not to praise God. Their immediate reaction was to "spread the word" (2:17). The shepherds became the first witnesses of the New Testament. Who was their audience? Surely, those at the inn, including the hotel manager, were the first to hear. "All who heard it were amazed" at the story (2:18). While Mary quietly reflected on the events of the past several months (2:19), the shepherds went back to work.

To give Christ glory and honor is a joy and privilege.

Perhaps they needed to return to the fields before their sheep wandered off. These faithful followers returned to their work, "glorifying and praising God" (2:20).

Everything had been "just as they had been told" (2:20). God is always faithful to keep his word. Joseph and Mary celebrated Christmas in quiet obedience. The angels proclaimed heavenly praise. The shepherds celebrated the birth by praising God and spreading the word.

Implications and Actions

The birth of Christ, into the world or into one's life, is cause for celebration and joy. Jesus brings change. He changed the world 2,000 years ago; he changes lives today. Whether in ways similar to the quiet obedience of Mary and Joseph, the ecstatic praise of angels, or the outspoken witness of the shepherds, we are to exalt and glorify the Christ of Christmas.

To give Christ glory and honor is a joy and privilege. I remember well *the year of the bike, the year of the tennis racket,* and *the year of the white Christmas.* But this year, let's return to the manger. This could be our greatest Christmas ever.

Do Not Fear!

The Bible is filled with numerous commands to *fear not,* including the statement to the shepherds (Luke 2:10). Even the greatest of leaders wrestle with fear. Here are a few examples of men and women God comforted with peace, the answer to fear. To each, God said, "Fear not."

- Abraham (Genesis 15:1)

- Moses (Numbers 21:34)

- Joshua (Joshua 8:1)

- Daniel (Daniel 10:12)

- Zechariah (Luke 1:13)

- Mary (Luke 1:30)

- Peter (Luke 5:10)

- Paul (Acts 27:23–24)

- John (Revelation 1:17–18)

Bringing It Home

- Identify your most meaningful Christmas, and plan to share the story with the class.

- The angel brought "good news of great joy" (Luke 2:10). List three ways you can express that joy.

- Consider ways you can emulate the shepherds, who "spread the word" (2:17).

- The title of today's lesson is "Glory to God!" Write down three ways you and your church can better glorify God this Christmas season.

Questions

1. How do you think the innkeeper responded to the shepherds' proclamation?

2. Which group's praise best fits your nature? Is it Mary and Joseph's, the angels', or the shepherds'?

3. Are you faithful to your call, as were the shepherds?

4. God burst onto the scene during the night shift for the shepherds. When was the last time God interrupted your routine in power and majesty?

Our Next New Study
(Available for use beginning March 2008)

1 AND 2 KINGS:
Leaders and Followers—Failed and Faithful

UNIT ONE. THE (SUPPOSED) GLORY DAYS (1 KINGS 1—11)

UNIT TWO. THE BROKEN KINGDOM (1 KINGS 12—16)

UNIT THREE. PROPHETS AT WORK (1 KINGS 17—2 KINGS 8)

UNIT FOUR. MISSING THE LAST CHANCE (2 KINGS 9—17)

UNIT FIVE. MISSING THE LAST CHANCE: THE SEQUEL (2 KINGS 18—25)

Lesson 11	When the Situation Is Desperate	2 Kings 18:1–19, 29–31; 19:1–11, 14–20
Lesson 12	The Only Hope	2 Kings 22:1—23:4
Lesson 13	The Bitter End	2 Kings 23:31–32, 36–37; 24:8–9, 18–20; 25:8–21
Easter Lesson	"Do Not Be Afraid"	Matthew 28:1–10

Additional Resources for Studying 1 and 2 Kings:[1]

A. Graeme Auld. *I and II Kings.* The Daily Study Bible. Louisville, Kentucky: Westminster John Knox Press, 1986.

M. Pierce Matheney, Jr., and Roy L. Honeycutt, Jr. "1 and 2 Kings." *The Broadman Bible Commentary.* Volume 3. Nashville, Tennessee: Broadman Press, 1970.

Richard D. Nelson. *1 and 2 Kings.* Interpretation: A Bible Commentary for Teaching and Preaching. Louisville, Kentucky: John Knox Press, 1987.

Choon-Leong Seow. "The First and Second Books of Kings." *The New Interpreter's Bible.* Volume III. Nashville: Abingdon Press, 1999.

NOTES

1. Listing a book does not imply full agreement by the writers or BAPTISTWAY with all of its comments.

How to Order More Bible Study Materials

It's easy! Just fill in the following information. For additional Bible study materials, see www.baptistwaypress.org or get a complete order form of available materials by calling 1-866-249-1799 or e-mailing baptistway@bgct.org.

Title of item	Price	Quantity	Cost
This Issue:			
Mark:Jesus' Works and Words—Study Guide (BWP001022)	$2.95	_____	_____
Mark:Jesus' Works and Words—Large Print Study Guide (BWP001023)	$3.15	_____	_____
Mark:Jesus' Works and Words—Teaching Guide (BWP001024)	$3.45	_____	_____
Additional Issues Available:			
Genesis 12—50: Family Matters—Study Guide (BWP000034)	$1.95	_____	_____
Genesis 12—50: Family Matters—Large Print Study Guide (BWP000032)	$1.95	_____	_____
Genesis 12—50: Family Matters—Teaching Guide (BWP000035)	$2.45	_____	_____
Leviticus, Numbers, Deuteronomy—Study Guide (BWP000053)	$2.35	_____	_____
Leviticus, Numbers, Deuteronomy—Large Print Study Guide (BWP000052)	$2.35	_____	_____
Leviticus, Numbers, Deuteronomy—Teaching Guide (BWP000054)	$2.95	_____	_____
Joshua, Judges—Study Guide (BWP000047)	$2.35	_____	_____
Joshua, Judges—Large Print Study Guide (BWP000046)	$2.35	_____	_____
Joshua, Judges—Teaching Guide (BWP000048)	$2.95	_____	_____
1 and 2 Samuel—Study Guide (BWP000002)	$2.35	_____	_____
1 and 2 Samuel—Large Print Study Guide (BWP000001)	$2.35	_____	_____
1 and 2 Samuel—Teaching Guide (BWP000003)	$2.95	_____	_____
Job, Ecclesiastes, Habakkuk, Lamentations: Dealing with Hard Times—Study Guide (BWP001016)	$2.75	_____	_____
Job, Ecclesiastes, Habakkuk, Lamentations: Dealing with Hard Times—Large Print Study Guide (BWP001017)	$2.85	_____	_____
Job, Ecclesiastes, Habakkuk, Lamentations: Dealing with Hard Times—Teaching Guide (BWP001018)	$3.25	_____	_____
Psalms and Proverbs: Songs and Sayings of Faith—Study Guide (BWP001000)	$2.75	_____	_____
Psalms and Proverbs: Songs and Sayings of Faith—Large Print Study Guide (BWP001001)	$2.85	_____	_____
Psalms and Proverbs: Songs and Sayings of Faith—Teaching Guide (BWP001002)	$3.25	_____	_____
Luke: Journeying to the Cross—Study Guide (BWP000057)	$2.35	_____	_____
Luke: Journeying to the Cross—Large Print Study Guide (BWP000056)	$2.35	_____	_____
Luke: Journeying to the Cross—Teaching Guide (BWP000058)	$2.95	_____	_____
The Gospel of John: The Word Became Flesh—Study Guide (BWP001008)	$2.75	_____	_____
The Gospel of John: The Word Became Flesh—Large Print Study Guide (BWP001009)	$2.85	_____	_____
The Gospel of John: The Word Became Flesh—Teaching Guide (BWP001010)	$3.25	_____	_____
Acts: Toward Being a Missional Church—Study Guide (BWP001013)	$2.75	_____	_____
Acts: Toward Being a Missional Church—Large Print Study Guide (BWP001014)	$2.85	_____	_____
Acts: Toward Being a Missional Church—Teaching Guide (BWP001015)	$3.25	_____	_____
Romans: What God Is Up To—Study Guide (BWP001019)	$2.95	_____	_____
Romans: What God Is Up To—Large Print Study Guide (BWP001020)	$3.15	_____	_____
Romans: What God Is Up To—Teaching Guide (BWP001021)	$3.45	_____	_____

1, 2 Timothy, Titus, Philemon—*Study Guide* (BWP000092)	$2.75	_____	_____
1, 2 Timothy, Titus, Philemon—*Large Print Study Guide* (BWP000091)	$2.85	_____	_____
1, 2 Timothy, Titus, Philemon—*Teaching Guide* (BWP000093)	$3.25	_____	_____
Hebrews and James—*Study Guide* (BWP000037)	$1.95	_____	_____
Hebrews and James—*Teaching Guide* (BWP000038)	$2.45	_____	_____
Revelation—*Study Guide* (BWP000084)	$2.35	_____	_____
Revelation—*Large Print Study Guide* (BWP000083)	$2.35	_____	_____
Revelation—*Teaching Guide* (BWP000085)	$2.95	_____	_____

Coming for use beginning March 2008

1 and 2 Kings: Leaders and Followers—*Study Guide* (BWP001025)	$2.95	_____	_____
1 and 2 Kings: Leaders and Followers—*Large Print Study Guide* (BWP001026)	$3.15	_____	_____
1 and 2 Kings: Leaders and Followers—*Teaching Guide* (BWP001027)	$3.45	_____	_____

Standard (UPS/Mail) Shipping Charges*	
Order Value	Shipping charge
$.01—$9.99	$6.00
$10.00—$19.99	$7.00
$20.00—$39.99	$8.00
$40.00—$79.99	$9.00
$80.00—$99.99	$12.00
$100.00—$129.99	$14.00
$130.00—$149.99	$18.00
$150.00—$199.99	$21.00
$200.00—$299.99	$26.00
$300.00 and up	10% of order value

Cost of items (Order value) _____
Shipping charges (see chart*) _____
TOTAL _____

*Plus, applicable taxes for individuals and other taxable entities (not churches) within Texas will be added. Please call 1-866-249-1799 if the exact amount is needed prior to ordering.

Please allow three weeks for standard delivery. For express shipping service: Call 1-866-249-1799 for information on additional charges.

_____   _____
YOUR NAME   PHONE

_____   _____
YOUR CHURCH   DATE ORDERED

_____
MAILING ADDRESS

_____   _____   _____
CITY   STATE   ZIP CODE

MAIL this form with your check for the total amount to
BAPTISTWAY PRESS, Baptist General Convention of Texas,
333 North Washington, Dallas, TX 75246-1798
(Make checks to "Baptist Executive Board.")

OR, **FAX** your order anytime to: 214-828-5376, and we will bill you.

OR, **CALL** your order toll-free: 1-866-249-1799
(M-Th 8:30 a.m.-8:30 p.m.; Fri 8:30 a.m.-5:00 p.m. central time),
and we will bill you.

OR, **E-MAIL** your order to our internet e-mail address:
baptistway@bgct.org, and we will bill you.

OR, **ORDER ONLINE** at www.baptistwaypress.org.

We look forward to receiving your order! Thank you!